CANADA

GREG CURNOE

CANADA

GREG CURNOE

XXXVII Esposizione Biennale Internazionale
d'Arte, Venezia, 1976
Organizzata dalla Galleria Nazionale del Canada,
Ottawa
Un Museo Nazionale del Canada

XXXVIIe Exposition biennale internationale
d'art, Venise, 1976
Organisée par la Galerie nationale du Canada,
Ottawa
Un des Musées nationaux du Canada

XXXVII International Biennial Exhibition of
Art, Venice, 1976
Organized by the National Gallery of Canada,
Ottawa
A National Museum of Canada

ⓒGalleria Nazionale del Canada
per l'Associazione dei Musei Nazionali del Canada
Ottawa, 1976
ⓒGalerie nationale du Canada
pour la Corporation des musées nationaux du Canada
Ottawa. 1976
ⓒThe National Gallery of Canada
for the Corporation of the National Museums of Canada
Ottawa, 1976

Testo del cat. no. 1 riprodotto con il permesso del Sig.
Greg Curnoe
Texte du cat. nº 1 reproduit avec la permission de M.
Greg Curnoe
Text accompanying cat. no. 1 reproduced courtesy of
Greg Curnoe

ISBN 0-88884-290-2
Stampato in Canada
Imprimé au Canada
Printed in Canada

INDICE
SOMMAIRE
CONTENTS

CANADA

GREG CURNOE

XXXVII Esposizione Biennale Internazionale
d'arte, Venezia, 1976

Mostra organizzata dalla Galleria Nazionale del
Canada, Ottawa
Un Museo Nazionale del Canada

PRESTATORI

The Alumni Association of the University of
Western Ontario, London, Ontario.

L'Artista, tramite The Isaacs Gallery, Toronto

La Banque d'art, Conseil des arts du Canada,
Ottawa

City Savings and Trust Company, Vancouver

Sig. E.J. Escaf, Lambeth, Ontario

Ontario Heritage Foundation, Toronto

Dottor M. Robinson, London, Ontario

PREFAZIONE

Questa è la dodicesima volta che il Canada partecipa alla Biennale di Venezia. In questa occasione, Pierre Théberge, Commissario della Provincia del Québec e Curatore presso la Galleria Nazionale del Canada, ha scelto le opere di un pittore della Provincia dell'Ontario, Greg Curnoe, e ha scritto di lui con ammirazione nel catalogo. L'organizzazione di questa mostra è stata molto avvantaggiata da cortesi prestiti di quadri provenienti da tanto lontano come dalla Columbia Britannica sulla costa occidentale del Canada. Questi prestiti hanno reso possibile alla Galleria Nazionale di esibire a Venezia gli esempi più probanti dell'opera di Curnoe. Come sempre, nell'esporre all'estero, la Gallerie Nazionale deve molto alla collaborazione della Divisione Affari Culturali del Ministero degli Affari Esteri del Canada, e in modo particolare all'aiuto dell'Ambasciata Canadese in Roma. È inoltre molto riconoscente per l'assistenza ricevuta dalla Ambasciata Italiana in Canada, di Ottawa.

Jean Sutherland Boggs
Direttrice
della Galleria Nazionale del Canada

INTRODUZIONE

Greg Curnoe vive a London, città di 225 mila abitanti, situata nel sud ovest della provincia dell'Ontario, che ospita un centro artistico molto attivo; egli è nato nel 1936.

Oltre ad essere pittore, Curnoe è anche scrittore, e tiene da anni dei diari personali[1] dove consegna regolarmente le sue osservazioni sulla sua vita quotidiana; ha anche fondato e diretto la rivista *Region* che venne pubblicata a London dal 1961 al 1967, e ha collaborato regolarmente alla rivista *20 Cents Magazine* che pure venne pubblicata a London dal 1966 al 1970.

Greg Curnoe ha anche fatto dei film[2].

Collezionista accanito, ha raccolto fra l'altro delle bottiglie di bevande non alcoliche fabbricate da piccole imprese in tutti gli angoli del Canada[3], carte geografiche del paese, biciclette e riviste di ciclismo, libri sui dirigibili e vari «Big Little Books»[4], strumenti topografici e una grande quantità di dischi di musica folcloristica contemporanea.

Greg Curnoe è anche corridore ciclista dilettante[5].

Si è appassionatamente interessato alla cultura popolare in tutte le sue manifestazioni, essendo membro attivo della «Associazione per la Documentazione degli Aspetti Negletti della Cultura in Canada» di cui fu, nel 1972, co-fondatore, e ha raccolto un'importante collezione di diapositive sull'arte popolare[6].

È anche membro di una cooperativa di alimentari e della «Forest City Art Gallery» di London, una cooperativa di artisti che è stata fondata nel

Figura I

dicembre del 1973. Fu anche fra i fondatori di tre altre cooperative: «The Garret Gallery» di Toronto, che funzionò dal 1957 al 1959, la «Region Gallery» di London che visse dal 1961 al 1963, e la «20/20 Gallery» che funzionò dal 1966 al 1970, pure a London.

Curnoe è inoltre attualmente il portavoce provinciale per l'Ontario del «CAR» *(Canadian Artists Representation)*, associazione nazionale di artisti canadesi. È stato fra i fondatori, ed è uno dei presidenti, del Partito Nichilista di London[7] che consacra tutte le sue risorse all'organizzazione di un pic-nic e di un banchetto annuale per i suoi membri. Il 1 luglio 1975 venne nominato artista in residenza presso la University Western of Ontario a London.

Musicista, Curnoe suona il «Kazoo» con la «Nihilist Spasm Band»[8], un'orchestra a effetti sonori che si è esibita regolarmente, il lunedì sera nelle birrerie di London a partire dal 1965, e che suona attualmente alla «Forest City Art Gallery».

Curnoe è un regionalista convinto e portavoce militante dell'anti-americanismo sistematico; e fu sotto questa bandiera che, con John Boyle, pittore di St. Catharines (Ontario), fu autore del manifesto *Refus continental* pubblicato nel 1969[9].

Greg Curnoe è sposato, e ha tre figli.

Tutta l'opera di Greg Curnoe è autobiografica. Egli ha scelto deliberatamente di circoscrivere alla sua regione, London nell'Ontario, le sue attività, ed è qui che in genere attinge i temi delle sue opere. Per Greg Curnoe non vi è cultura possibile che non sia regionale, non vi è arte possibile che non abbia la sua origine immediata nell'esperienza quotidiana. La sua pittura è spontanea, senza programmi sistematici, e ci si ritrova, tutto quello che per un motivo o un altro, attrae la sua attenzione al momento. Greg Curnoe si considera un artigiano, un maestro di tutti i mestieri, un osservatore soggettivo della realtà. È mosso da un solo principio: il piacere che prova nel fare quello che fa. Greg Curnoe vuole che la sua arte faccia parte integrale della sua vita, e che rifletta quanto più possibile tutto quello che lo interessa[10].

Lo studio che occupa attualmente dal 1968, ha otto finestre divise su tre delle quattro pareti (fig. I). I quadri che sono presentati qui corrispondono a queste otto finestre, e si aggiungono ad una lunga serie, iniziata nel 1961, di opere che descrivono quello che egli vedeva dalle finestre dei due studi che hanno preceduto l'attuale. Queste opere riflettono un atteggiamento comune, quello di un benevolo esame della realtà come è stata inquadrata dal capriccio della costruzione[11].

NOTE

1. La casa editrice Coach House Press di Toronto sta preparando un'edizione in facsimile di cinque volumi di uno di questi diari, *The Blue Book,* scritto dall'agosto 1964 al marzo 1967. L'edizione di un altro, *The Coke Book,* è in preparazione presso l'Alphabet Press di London. Curnoe tiene anche un «diario sonoro» su cassette. Fece la sua prima registrazione il 19 marzo 1968 in occasione di un viaggio in automobile fatto assieme al poeta Robert Fones, da London a Montréal.
2. Ha girato due film:
Sowesto, 1947 – 1969, film di 16 mm a colori, muto, 30 minuti.
Connexions, 1969 – 1970, 16 mm a colori, sonoro, 15 minuti.

3. Queste bottiglie sono, fra l'altro, importanti per Curnoe perché dimostrano l'esistenza di culture regionali in Canada. La forma delle bottiglie, il disegno dei marchi di fabbrica variano da una regione all'altra, e anche il sapore di una stessa composizione, «cream soda» o «bière d'épinette», per esempio, non è eguale secondo la marca o il luogo d'origine, il ché è indizio di assai precise preferenze regionali.

4. Libri illustrati per bambini, pubblicati principalmente durante gli anni quaranta.

Curnoe ha illustrato con 194 disegni il libro di David McFadden, *The Great Canadian Sonnet* pubblicato in due volumi nel 1970, in conformità ai principi e al formato dei «Big Little Books». La presentazione caratteristica di questo genere di opera, illustrazioni inquadrate da un margine nero e accompagnate da una didascalia permetteva ai bambini di «leggere» il libro indipendentemente dal testo.

5. Se nell'autunno 1973 ha vinto il trofeo del club di ciclismo, i «London Centennial Wheelers», non è per i suoi meriti di ciclista ma per l'assiduità alle corse settimanali del club. D'altronde è stato lui a disegnare e far confezionare nel 1975 la màglia dei membri del club.

Prima di aver terminato le vedute dalle otto finestre del suo studio di Weston Street, Curnoe fece, nel 1972, una serie di «ritratti» di due delle sue biciclette, una la «C.C.M. 1951» e l'altra, la «Zeus», all'acrilico su legno compensato ritagliato secondo la sagoma della macchina. Nel 1973 iniziò un'altra serie di questi «ritratti» di tutte le sue biciclette, sempre a grandezza naturale, ma questa volta ad acquarello su carta rettangolare. Nello stesso anno l'artista commincia anche una terza serie di «ritratti», di ruote da bicicletta su carta quadrata.

6. Secondo il suo manifesto, questa associazione ha per scopo di «sconvolgere l'artificiosa frontiera fra «belle» arti e cultura»; si propone di pubblicare un giorno i documenti fotografici che sta accumulando. Pierre Théberge ne è co-fondatore e co-presidente. L'Associazione ha presentato dal 6 dicembre 1974 al 2 gennaio 1975 più di 600 diapositive di oggetti «trascurati» presso la Public Library and Art Museum di London nell'Ontario, e in questa occasione ha pubblicato il primo numero della sua rivista.

7. La parola «NO» ([trad.]: non) è l'unico programma del Partito Nichilista. Tutti i suoi membri ne sono contemporaneamente presidenti.

8. Il «Kazoo» è uno strumento a fiato.

La «Nihilist Spasm Band», ha inciso un disco nel 1968 per la Casa Allied Record Corporation di Toronto; questa orchestra ha anche suonato a Parigi durante la «VI Biennale des Jeunes» e all'«Institute of Contemporary Art» di Londra nell'ottobre 1969. L'orchestra contava, oltre a Curnoe, altri sei musicisti: John B. Boyle, William A. Exley, Murray Favro, Archie Leitch, Hugh McIntyre e Art Pratten. Ad eccezione dei tamburi, l'orchestra ha inventato i propri strumenti musicali.

9. Il titolo del manifesto parafrasa il *Refus Global* di Paul-Émile Borduas pubblicato nell'agosto 1948.

Questo atteggiamento gli ha tuttavia causato delle noie quando si è rivelato nelle sue opere: fra l'altro una pittura murale, commissionata nel 1967 dal governo canadese per l'aeroporto di Dorval non venne mai istallata a motivo del suo anti-americanismo (la pittura si trova nei depositi della Galleria Nazionale); un progetto ordinatogli da una società di tabacchi per un murale destinato a essere dipinto su un edificio di Toronto, fu rifiutato per le stesse ragioni. Curnoe rifiuta di esporre negli Stati Uniti.

10. Bruce Kidd: «Hai l'intenzione di preservare ogni istante della tua vita?»

Greg Curnoe: «Prima di tutto io non preservo ogni istante, non lo potrei fare. Questo vorrebbe dire che tutte le mie ore di veglia sarebbero occupate da questa opera di conservazione. Io faccio solamente quello che mi interessa.» Traduzione dall'inglese: «Bruce Kidd intervista Greg Curnoe», nel *The Canadian Forum,* tomo LIII, No. 631 (agosto 1973), pag. 22.

11. Lo studio che occupò in Richmond Street a London dal 1960 al 1963 non aveva che due finestre; Curnoe stampigliò con un alfabeto di timbri di gomma, su di un pezzo di tela da ricalco (cm. 48,2 x cm. 35,5) una descrizione del paesaggio urbano visto dalla finestra di sinistra sulla parete ovest. Si tratta del *Cityscape* che fa parte della collezione del Signor David P. Silcox e signora di Ottawa.

Lo studio che occupò in seguito in King Street, dal 1963 al 1968, contava sette finestre; egli descrisse sistematicamente nei suoi quadri quello che vedeva da ciascuna di esse.

CATALOGO

1

*Veduta dell'Ospedale Victoria, seconda serie
(10 febbraio 1969 – 10 marzo 1971)*

Olio, inchiostro da timbri, grafite e carta da parati
su legno compensato, metallo, plexiglas, alto-parlanti, nastro sonoro magnetico e testo stampato su
un quaderno di otto pagine (Testo originale re-
prodotto alle pagine 58 – 65.)
cm. 243,8 x cm. 487,0
ESPOSIZIONE: Toronto, The Issacs Gallery, 17
marzo – 5 aprile 1971, *Greg Curnoe Views of
Victoria Hospital and Wings over the Atlantic.*
COLLEZIONE: GALLERIA NAZIONALE DEL CANADA,
OTTAWA
Acquistato nel 1971

Esistono altre quatro opere sullo stesso tema della
*Veduta dell'Ospedale Victoria, seconda serie (10
febbraio 1969 – 10 marzo 1971):* l'una è costituita
dalla descrizione del paesaggio, scritta con un
alfabeto di timbri di gomma, su sei tele consecutive di cm. 299,7 x cm. 238,7 ciascuna[12], la seconda e la terza sono due registrazioni al magnetofono[13], e l'ultima è un collage[14].
   Curnoe ha provvisto anche, a intervalli regolari
dal 1969, a registrare un'altra descrizione del paesaggio visto tuttavia attraverso la finestra situata
immediatamente a destra del centro della parete

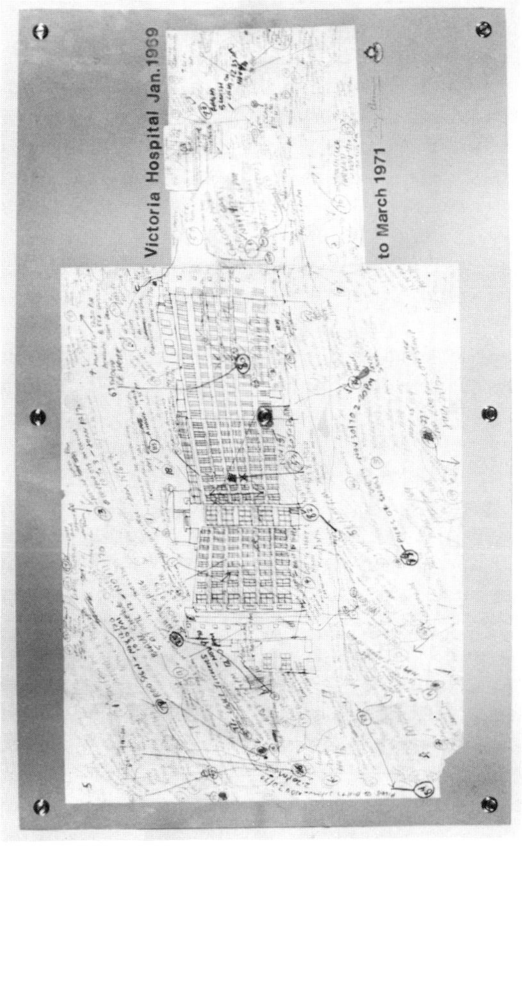

Figura II

a nord del suo studio (quella del No. 8 di questa mostra), su un terminal (una macchina per scrivere), collegato per telefono a un ordinatore del dipartimento delle Scienze dell'Informazione dell' «University of Western Ontario» a London[15] (fig. III).

Durante i due anni che ha impiegato a dipingere il quadro, Curnoe ha notato, in ordine cronologico, su di un foglio di carta sul quale aveva fatto un disegno schematico dell'ospedale nel constesto del paesaggio (fig. II), quello che ha potuto osservare casualmente nelle ore che ha passato a guardare fuori della finestra.

La Veduta dell'Ospedale Victoria, seconda serie (10 febbraio 1969 – 10 marzo 1971), è composta dall'aggiunta di tre elementi di natura differente che servono a descrivere la scena a tre livelli di percezione: un quadro, un testo e una trama sonora. Il quadro serve come punto di convergenza per gli altri due elementi: i numeri sparpagliati sulla superficie trovano il loro significato nel testo che Curnoe ha dattilografato in un quaderno che corrisponde esattamente agli appunti accumulati sullo schizzo; la trama sonora viene intesa a partire dai due alto-parlanti situati alle estremità superiori del quadro. Durante la percezione dell'intera opera, lo spettatore è indotto a passare costantemente da un livello all'altro per ricreare, attraverso la percezione spontanea degli elementi visivi, scritti e sonori, non solamente il paesaggio nei suoi dettagli, ma anche il disordine degli avvenimenti che hanno avuto luogo durante la produzione dell'opera da parte di Curnoe.

Alla vista del quadro, come alla lettura del testo, si induce nella mente quasi sempre, e in modo assolutamente naturale, un fluire di passaggi da un senso all'altro, e spesso anche nell'interno stesso di un dettaglio; anche se è letterale, la trama sonora non sfugge affatto a questa regola dell'ambiguità dei significati.

Poiché questi tre elementi si presentano simultaneamente, ciascuno di essi non raggiunge il suo pieno significato che collegato agli altri due. L'analisi di un elemento visuale, per esempio, ci conduce per forza a considerare l'elemento letterale, che può alle volte spiegarlo. Ed é vero anche il contrario.

Sul quadro domina l'edificio annunciato dal titolo. Il testo in sé non c'insegna nulla di più sulla sua funzione di ospedale; se Curnoe l'ha dipinto così grande è perché domina il paesaggio reale[16]. L'edificio è circondata da alberi, da case, da campi e da altre costruzioni. Alla sua sinistra, sul quadro, c'è una bottiglia, alla destra un aeroplano. Una fascia di colore, principalmente rosa e viola, divide la composizione in due parti quasi eguali, e rappresenta la crocera della finestra[17]. I numeri in superficie rappresentano l'ordine cronologico del testo, che a sua volta, rappresenta avvenimenti che si sono effettivamente verificati, ma che non sono rappresentati, in genere, da un'immagine dipinta sul quadro[18].

Salvo questa eccezione, ogni macchia di colore rappresenta qualche cosa che esisteva realmente nel paesaggio, sul vetro stesso della finestra, oppure nello studio, come la bottiglia. Ognuno di questi elementi visivi ha un'importanza primordiale per Greg Curnoe perché, secondo lui, non si può veramente conoscere l'insieme di una cosa che esaminandola, in primo luogo, in tutte le sue parti; così, tutto quanto si trova nello sfondo e che, nella realtà dovrebbe essere sfumato, è qui rappresentato altrettanto distintamente che se fosse in primo piano. Questa «mania» del dettaglio lo induce, per esempio, a dipingere una ad una le 218 finestre visibili sulla facciata dell'ospedale! In lui è un atteggiamento che corrisponde a quella passione per i dettagli tipica di certi pittori naïf.

La scelta dei colori è arbitraria, e la loro funzione non è sempre realistica: così l'ospedale, che in realtà è composto di mattoni gialli, passa qui, fra l'altro, dal giallo al rosa, quindi al verde pallido e all'arancione, e gli alberi sono verdi o gialli, rosa o blu. Come a confermare questo atteggiamento nei confronti del colore, il numero 55 del testo ci avverte comunque che l'albero, qui dipinto in rosa, è in realtà divenuto improvvisamente giallo arancio chiaro. Questo sistema è giustificato in Curnoe dall'intuizione che ha della funzione stessa del colore che è quella di «colorare», senza necessariamente dover corrispondere alla realtà ordinaria; gli basta che serva a distinguere le forme l'una dall'altra, e soprattutto che corrisponda si suoi gusti[19].

Tutto il quadro, perfino nella sua struttura, funziona come la finestra che gli è servita da punto di partenza: è un oggetto di fronte al quale ci si piazza, e attraverso il quale si vede simultaneamente un'immagine e la superficie sulla quale questa immagine è vista. Mentre i numeri 5, 36, 37, 67, e 97 del testo sottintendono la trasparenza del vetro, la solidità della sua superficie e il suo potere di riflettere la notte, il numero 58 conferma chiaramente questa metafora della superficie del quadro in quanto finestra: la goccia d'acqua menzionata nel testo è rappresentata dalla traccia di una goccia di pittura dipinta deliberatamente dall'alto in basso sulla superficie del quadro[20], come se questa avesse in qualche modo la trasparenza della finestra. che il quadro sia anche, in modo molto più diretto, nient'altro che una superficie solida e opaca, è, altrettanto chiaramente, indicato nel testo ai numeri 3 e 80[21].

Le annotazioni del testo sono dirette e prosaiche, e dipendono interamente dal suo umore del momento. Esse sono altrettanto poco sistematiche che il quadro stesso: è un racconto composto di frammenti, e gli avvenimenti hanno, di per sé, dettato il suo svolgimento. È il loro coincidere coll'attenzione visiva di Curnoe che costituisce il punto di partenza del testo.

I raggruppamenti tematici che possiamo fare leggendo, possono trovare una spiegazione che è spesso altrettanto prosaica degli avvenimenti stessi: per esempio, se Curnoe osserva ai numeri 12, 14, 16, 20, 39, 40, 41, 42, 43, 44, 51, 54, 65, 68, 69, 72, 73, 78, 90 e 97 tante luci, è perché non è facile vedere altre cose, attraverso la finestra, di notte; così, se parla più di una volta delle nuvole (25, 48, 57) di fumi (6, 11, 15, 25, 32, 47, 66, 77, 88, 93, 98, 106, 111, 116), di uccelli (22, 33, 52, 95, 96, 107, 113), o di insetti (19, 34, 35, 50), è perché non è possibile vedere altro se ci si mette ad osservare quello che succede nell'atmosfera!

Nei numeri 3, 7, 28, 37, 38, 51, 53, 63, 64, 78, 81, 92, 94, 104 e 105, Curnoe non fa altro che menzionare dei nomi di persone senza spiegare veramente a chi appartengono, salvo un'eccezione[22] questo perché il testo è anche un diario personale, e l'autore non sente il bisogno di descrivere l'esatta posizione di queste persone nella sua vita ogni volta che ne parla. Poiché questo testo è ormai pubblico, non è forse senza interesse conoscere a chi corrispondano questi nomi nell'ordine del loro apparire nel testo: Owen

Curnoe è il figlio primogenito dell'artista; Jack (Chambers) è un pittore[23]; Jimmy (McRae) è un vicino di casa; Glen (Curnoe) è suo fratello cadetto, bibliotecario[24]; Archie (Leitch) è un contabile, e a quel tempo musicista col «Nihilist Spasm Band»; C(lare) B(ice) è anche lei pittrice[25]; Sheila (Curnoe) è la moglie di Greg, e Galen[26], suo figlio minore; Selwyn (Dewney) è un esperto della pittografia degli Indiani del Canada[27] e Irene è sua moglie, terapeuta a mezzo delle arti e donna politica; Mary (Rose) è ceramista; Doreen (Curry) è una bibliotecaria specializzata in musica; Hal (Sheftel) era impiegato presso una ditta di Toronto che noleggia proiettori; infine Sam, lui, è un gatto della famiglia Curnoe che da allora è scomparso!

Dire chi sono, anche in breve, queste persone col descriverne soprattutto la funzione, serve a spiegare un poco il senso della loro presenza nella vita di Greg Curnoe; una biografia più dettagliata di ciascuno di loro, anche se non corrispondesse alle intenzioni di Curnoe all'epoca in cui annotò il loro nome, servirebbe a definire più precisamente l'ambiente culturale nel quale si evolve.

Il testo è, nel suo insieme, una cronaca del tempo che scorre, e ogni annotazione è identificata a mezzo della data e dell'ora in cui è stata registrata. L'accumulo paziente di tutti questi dettagli finisce per ricostruire, poco a poco, la vita del pittore nei momenti in cui era seduto davanti alla finestra e annotava quello che vedeva, quello che sentiva, oppure ciò che accadeva altrove all'infuori dello studio o del paesaggio. È il caso dei numeri 104 e 105, e per questo motivo essi non sono dipinti sulla superficie.

Il testo potrebbe essere commentato numero per numero, frase per frase, parola per parola, anche, e un'analisi di questo genere ricreerebbe, come una ricostruzione archeologica, tutto un ambiente, tutta un'epoca. Ci farebbe conoscere, ad esempio, che tempo faceva alla tale ora o il tale giorno[28], come erano illuminati gli edifici, le strade, lo studio, che genere di musica potevamo sentire[29], come la gente comunicava[30], come si muoveva, ecc.

Queste annotazioni, proprio perché sono assolutamente banali, creano per accumulo una somma di vita quotidiana. Questo testo, come la memoria, costituisce un insieme le cui parti componenti possono, prese da sole, essere più o meno significative, ma ritrovano in pieno il loro senso nella loro convergenza verso un centro. Il testo trova un primo significato nella sua totalizzazione, un altro nella sua convergenza col quadro, e un altro, infine, per quanto rivela dell'individualità dell'autore che è il suo punto d'origine.

La trama sonora è il solo elemento letterale della composizione. La scelta della collocazione del microfono è fatta ad una data e a un'ora precisa (come indicano i numeri 26, 27, 28, 29, e 31 del testo), e i rumori che si sentono si sono, in genere, presentati per caso[31]. Curnoe ha scelto a suo piacere quale delle colonne sonore doveva far parte della composizione, e due delle cinque colonne registrate vennero distrutte per la sola ragione della loro cattiva qualità tecnica. Per il suo assoluto realismo, la trama sonora ricollega l'opera al tempo e al luogo della sua creazione. È soprattutto per questo che questa *Veduta dell'Ospedale Victoria, seconda serie (10 febbraio 1969 – 10 marzo 1971)* è precisata per sempre[32].

Fu mentre dipingeva il quadro, che Greg Curnoe ebbe improvvisamente l'idea di stampigliare colla parola *Region* la finestra attraverso la quale aveva guardato per tanto tempo. Questo gesta ha differenti significati: è anzitutto e soprattutto ironia da parte dell'artista. E anche un modo semplice di confondere in qualche maniera qualsiasi distinzione fra l'arte e la realtà «ordinaria». Curnoe ha in seguito ripetuto la stampiglia sul quadro, questa volta sottolineandola con la sua firma anche essa stampigliata, perchè faceva allora parte logica del soggetto da ritrarre. Questa appare su cinque dei sette quadri di questa mostra, perchè si è trovata sulle finestre corrispondenti a questi.

La parola *Region* sul quadro è anche un modo per definire l'opera: questo quadro, questo testo, questa trama sonora, costituiscono, frammento per frammento, il ritratto di una regione e al tempo stesso quello dell'autore dell'opera.

NOTE

12. *Veduta dell'Ospedale Victoria no. 1 a 6 (27 agosto 1968 – 10 gennaio 1969)*. Collezione della Galleria Nazionale del Canada, Ottawa. Nel fare la seconda serie, l'artista si è sforzato di includere quasi tutto quello che aveva descritto nella prima serie, mentre copriva collo sguardo lo stresso panorama.

13. *Veduta dell'Ospedale Victoria no. 1, terza serie (16 aprile 1969, 11.45 del mattino alle 12.15, e 17 aprile 1969 dalle 8.40 alle 9.10)*. Registrazione stereofonica su cassetta (collezione dell'artista). Greg Curnoe, nel catalogo della mostra *955,000*, organizzata da Lucy R. Lippard, e presentata presso la «Vancouver Art Gallery» dal 13 gennaio all'8 febbraio 1970, da delle informazione su questa registrazione: «Il microfono venne

piazzato su di una scatola di legno, sul bordo delle vecchia sponda del fiume a 41° 8′ a nord dell'angolo nord-ovest della nostra casa...» (traduzione dall'inglese).

Esiste un'altra versione di questa registrazione; questa, fatta nella primavera del 1969, fu presentata in una mostra del gruppo *The London Survey* alla «20/20 Gallery» di London dal 22 aprile all'11 maggio 1969.

14. *Veduta dell'Ospedale Victoria, quarta serie (1970 – 1971)*. Collezione dell'artista. Collage su di un pezzo di plexiglas ritagliato secondo la sagoma dell'ospedale.

15. L'ordinatore elettronico è stato programmato in modo da poter ritrasmettere gli scritti di Curnoe esattamente alla stessa cadenza (con gli stessi errori di battuta, le stesse esitazioni) alla quale li aveva registrati in partenza. E con l'entusiastico appoggio di John Hart, direttore del dipartimento delle Scienze dell'Informazione dell'«University of Western Ontario» che Bill Frazer e Mike Dawdy hanno redatto il programma dell'ordinatore.

Curnoe ha presentato due pagine del suo diario come vennero ritrasmesse dall'ordinatore elettronico per telefono interurbano a un terminale nell'esposizione *45° 30′N – 73° 36′W* presso l'Università «Sir George Williams» e al «The Saidye Bronfman Centre» a Montréal dall'1 al 17 febbraio 1971. Il testo di Curnoe nel catalogo spiega brevemente il progetto.

16. È di nuovo il caso che è, in qualche modo, responsabile della presenza di questo ospedale nella sua opera. Esso è infatti visibile da tutte le finestre della parete a nord del suo studio, ma non è per l'ospedale che egli ha comperato lo studio! Curnoe ha già pensato, ironicamente, ad una ana-

logia fra l'Ospedale «Victoria» nella sua opera e il «Montagne Sainte-Victoire» di Cézanne!

17. Curnoe d'altronde ha dimenticato di dipingere il montante della finestra; è solo all'ultimo momento che si è reso conto che esso aveva occupato il suo campo di vista per più di due anni! Non è, d'altra parte, neppure indicata nello schizzo della collezione di Anne Brodsky di Toronto (fig. II).

18. Pertanto vi è un'eccezione al realismo tel testo, il numero 24, che spiega la presenza dell'aeroplano militare americano in fiamme nel cielo di London; Curnoe ha deliberatamente presentato questo avvenimento fittizio come se fosse realmente accaduto per costringere lo spettatore a chiedersi se fosse vero, a considerarne la possibilità.

19. Curnoe non ha mai veramente smentito questa diceria, certamente malevola, che è corsa nella sua famiglia e negli ambienti artistici di London, cioé la pretesa che fosse daltonico; è questo il suo modo li affermare il suo libero arbitrio in fatto di colori, e rappresenta il suo rifiuto di accordare a questi qualsiasi valore obiettivo (di riferirsi al colore «reale» delle cose).

20. Questa striscia dipinta passa dal rosa pallido al giallo, e quindi al bianco cremoso; le altre strisce che si trovano qua e là sulla superficie, sono accidentali.

21. Questo perpetuo oscillare fra la «realtà» e il quadro, questo andirivieni visuale e letterario fra tautologia e metafora, sono intuitivamente dimostrati dall'impiego della parola *qui* nel testo.

Mentre nei numeri 3 e 80, *qui* indica solamente quello che si trova *sulla* superficie del quadro (che è *qui* nel momento in cui la guardiamo), si riferisce prevalentemente ai numeri 7, 38 e 92, a quello che avviene in realtà *laggiù,* nell'ospedale, ai numeri 95 e 96, *laggiù* nel paesaggio reale.

Il significato di *qui* al numero 21 è ancora più ambiguo perché indica lo studio e il terreno su cui sorge, piuttosto che il frammento di paesaggio al di sopra del quale è posto il numero.

Al numero 37, *qui* indica simultaneamente sia la finestra che il paesaggio.

22. Il nome di *Jean Béliveau* che appare al numero 67, appartiene a un celebre giocatore di hockey del Club Canadien di Montréal; esso serve come marca di fabbrica per un giocattolo da bambini che si trova nello studio dell'artista.

23. Chambers d'altra parte ha dipinto, nel 1969 – 1970, una veduta realistica dell'Ospedale Victoria in un paesaggio invernale, partendo da una fotografia a colore che aveva scattato dal tetto dello studio di Curnoe. È un quadro la cui atmosfera silenziosa e malinconica è l'antitesi del quadro di Curnoe.

24. W. Glen Curnoe è anche l'autore di *Around London 1900–1950, A Picture of History,* London, presso l'autore, 1973.

25. Clare Bice è anche l'ex-conservatore della «London Public Library and Art Gallery» (Ontario).

26. I due incidenti dei numeri 104 e 105 furono particolarmente sfortunati par Galen, perché avvennero a due giorni uno dall'altro quando aveva tre anni.

27. Selwyn Dewney è l'autore con Kenneth E. Kidd di *Indian Rock Paintings of the Great Lakes,* Toronto, University of Toronto Press, 1967.

28. Le quattro stagioni di ciascuno dei due anni sono anche rappresentate simultaneamente sul quadro.

29. Al numero 118 *Syrinx* è il nome di un gruppo di tre musicisti, John Mills Cockell, Doug Pringle, e Allan Wells. Il disco che hanno inciso sotto il nome «True North» a Toronto nel 1970, s'intitola anche *Syrinx*; ed è di questo che si tratta. Syrinx ha anche inciso *Long Lost Relative* presso la «True North» nel 1971.

30. Vedere i numeri 18, 37, 38, 53, 63, 64, 78, 79, 81 e 92.

31. Vi sono alcune eccezioni: colpi di bacchette su un coperchio di metallo davanti al microfono, a sinistra, e poi su quello a destra, e dei colpi di pistola-giocattolo che seguono dappresso i rumori di aeroplano dovuti al caso.

32. La prima parte della cassetta stereofonica di 120 minuti corrispone, con una leggera variante nell'ora della registrazione, al numero 28 del testo, e la seconda parte al numero 29. Curnoe ha scritto sulla cassetta: «Microfono sul divisorio direttamente sotto due camini – quale si vede dalla finestra a nord-ovest, dalle ore 8.15 di sera alle 9.15, 9 agosto 1970, 10, 25 di sera alle 11. 25, 16 agosto 1970» (traduzione dall'inglese).

Curnoe ha l'intenzione di sostituire questa registrazione collegando il quadro in mostra nella Galleria Nazionale di Ottawa, direttamente per telefono a un microfono che verrebbe piazzato nello stesso posto dietro lo studio.

2

Veduta dalla finestra più a nord sulla parete di levante (15 marzo 1969 – 17 settembre 1969)

Acrilico, inchiostro da timbri, carta da parati su legno compensato, alto-parlante e nastro sonoro magnetico.

cm. 226,0 x cm. 256,5 (massima dimensione, incluso l'alto-parlante)

ESPOSIZIONE: Toronto, The Isaacs Gallery, 17 marzo – 5 aprile 1971, *Greg Curnoe Views of Victoria Hospital and Wings over the Atlantic.*

DONO DEL SIG. J. H. MOORE E SIGNORA ALL'ONTARIO FOUNDATION HERITAGE

Le scritte stampigliate sulla superficie del quadro indicano dove e quando gli oggetti ritratti sono stati comprati a London: «Hugh's Kazoo» è però uno strumento musicale costruito da Hugh McIntyre, membro anche lui del «Nihilist Spasm Band» rimasto nello studio dell'artista dopo che lo «Nihilist Spasm Band» si trasferì nelle birrerie di London dove suona, più o meno settimanalmente, dal 1965.

La forma del quadro viene dal fatto che è stato costruito con pezzi di compensato rimasti nello studio dopo che Curnoe, nel 1967 – 1968, ebbe costruito l'oggetto a forma di piramide chiamato *Kamikaze.*

L'alto-parlante diffonde dei rumori registrati all'esterno, sotto la finestra il 19 giugno 1969 dalle 1.30 alle 2.30 del pomeriggio, e dalle 9 alle 10 di sera. La carta da parati che Curnoe utilizza per tutti i quadri di questa mostra, è una carta collata del commercio, un prodotto di uso domestico scelto per le sue qualità comuni.

3

Veduta dalla finestra la più ad est sulla parete a nord (5 maggio 1969 – 18 dicembre 1969)

Acrilico, inchiostro da timbri, carta da parati su legno compensato, alto-parlante e nastro sonoro magnetico
cm. 274,3 x cm. 122,0 (alto-parlante incluso)
ESPOSIZIONE: Toronto, The Isaacs Gallery, 17 marzo – 5 aprile 1971, *Greg Curnoe Views of Victoria Hospital and Wings over the Atlantic.*
COLLEZIONE: L'ARTISTA E THE ISAACS GALLERY, TORONTO

La posizione dell'alto-parlante sopra al quadro corrisponde, press'a poco, a quella del microfono sospeso dal soffitto dello studio durante la registrazione della trama sonora, dalle 11.15 di mattina alle 12.13 di venerdì, 16 maggio 1969, e dalle 1.55 pomeridiane alle 3.55 di sabato, 17 maggio 1969. Un'altra colonna sonora, registrata il 30 luglio 1970 alle 1.41 del pomeriggio e alle 2.30, non fu utilizzata per questo quadro.

L'oggetto identificato colla parola «EVERLAST» è un casco da boxeur, e la forma che occupa il centro in basso rappresenta la tromba di un vecchio grammofono che Curnoe ha utilizzato per costruire uno dei suoi «kazoo».

Curnoe ammira particolarmente la semplicità e l'immediatezza degli scritti dello scienziato svizzero Auguste Piccard, e la citazione stampigliata in basso e a destra del quadro, è la traduzione di uno di questi testi ricavato da *Entre terre et ciel,* edizioni Ouchy, Losanna, 1946: «Al di sopra dell'orizzonte, il cielo. Prima la troposfera vista in tutta la sua estensione, lattea, quasi bianca sull'immediato orizzonte. Un po' più in alto, il cielo, come lo conosciamo. Ancora più in alto è nettamente visibile la tropopausa, limite fra troposfera e stratosfera. Più in alto ancora, la stratosfera. Essa si stacca nettamente dalla trosposfera per la sua perfetta limpidezza. È azzurra, di un blu carico, sempre più scuro più si solleva lo sguardo. Più in alto diventa violacea. Noi abbiamo già osservato questo colore vermiglio della stratosfera, la mattina molto presto o la sera, quando, per l'osservatore terrestre, il sole è ancora sotto all'orizzonte. Solamente la stratosfera è illuminata, ma non è colore azzurro cielo, ma una mescolanza di azzurro e di rosso.» (Pagg. 129–130.)

4

Veduta dalla finestra più a sud sulla parete a est (10 novembre 1969 – gennaio 1970)

Acrilico, inchiostro da timbri, carta da parati su legno compensato, alto-parlante e nastro sonoro magnetico
cm. 71,1 x cm. 208,3
ESPOSIZIONE: Toronto, The Isaacs Gallery, 17 marzo – 5 aprile 1971, *Greg Curnoe Views of Victoria Hospital and Wings over the Atlantic.*
COLLEZIONE: SIG. E. J. ESCAF, LAMBETH, ONTARIO

Il legno utilizzato nella costruzione di questo quadro proviene da una cassa de imballaggio. I testi tutti stampigliati e ci descrivano gli oggetti che sono effettivamente situati vicino alla finestra, nello studio. Dall'alto in basso si legge (trad.): «Sony F99S/ microfono»; quindi «Fotografia superiore in bianco e nero di Len's Brough su cartolina postale»; seguito de «Girata di un assegno della B(anca) di M(ontreal) con una annotazione a matita sulla fiera dei «bricoleurs» e su Walt Disney»; poi «Lettera manoscritta di R(ichard) Hamilton con istruzioni per Highgate»; e infine «Morandi, calendario Olivetti, 1967».

La scritta *more trivia/no allegory again!!* ([trad.]: ancora banalità, per ora nessuna ispirazione!!) è un ironico commento dell'artista sulla veduta dalla finestra e sugli oggetti che dipinge, ed esprime anche il suo profondo disgusto dell'allegoria e dei tentativi di trovare un senso «profondo» nella sua arte.

La parola seguita dalle fréccie *ASA* è il nome di una gatta della famiglia Curnoe che venne uccisa da un'automobile durante la realizzazione del quadro.

La trama sonora di 60 minuti venne registrata alle 11.50 di sera il 2 dicembre 1969 (Curnoe che parla della gatta) e alle 9.55 o alle 10.55 la sera del 3 dicembre 1969 (una partita di hockey trasmessa da Toronto da una radio posta in alto a destra della finestra).

5

Veduta dalla finestra a sinistra del centro, sulla parete a nord (23 giugno – 21 agosto 1970)

Acrilico, inchiostro da timbri, carta da parati su legno compensato, alto-parlante e nastro sonoro magnetico

cm. 187,0 x cm. 171,5 (alto-parlante incluso)

ESPOSIZIONE: Toronto, The Isaacs Gallery, 17 marzo – 5 aprile 1971, *Greg Curnoe Views of Victoria Hospital and Wings over the Atlantic.*

COLLEZIONE: THE ALUMNI ASSOCIATION OF THE UNIVERSITY OF WESTERN ONTARIO, LONDON, ONTARIO

Il pezzo di carta ritratto al centro del quadro è un menù del ristorante Mackie's situato sulla spiaggia di Port Stanley, sul Lago Erie, vicino a London, Ontario; questo ristorante è dipinto con un motivo arancione e blu che a Curnoe piace molto.

Il testo spiega come è stato rotto il vetro della finestra (trad.): «Come si è rotta la finestra? Avevo appoggiato l'ultima sezione della persiana di legno blu contro il caminetto perché il giovane vicino aveva camminato sopra nel prato! La persiana deve essere stata spinta dal vento o si deve essere rovesciata e cadendo ha rotto il vetro! Scritto il 20 agosto 1970 – ore 15.10».

La trama sonora è stata registrata piazzando il microfono all'esterno, su uno sgabello, a destra della finestra, il 20 agosto 1970 dalle ore 10 alle 11 di sera, e il 23 agosto 1970 dalle 5.40 alle 6.40 del mattino. Curnoe ha anche rotto un vetro durante le registrazione.

6

Veduta dalla finestra la più a nord sulla parete ovest (22 ottobre 1970 – 10 marzo 1971)

Acrilico, inchiostro da timbri, carta da parati su legno compensato, alto-parlanti e nastro sonoro magnetico
cm. 122,0 x cm. 304,8
ESPOSIZIONE: Toronto, The Isaacs Gallery, 17 marzo – 5 aprile 1971, *Greg Curnoe Views of Victoria Hospital and Wings over the Atlantic.*
COLLEZIONE: DOTTOR M. ROBINSON, LONDON, ONTARIO

Le bottiglie dipinte in basso del quadro fanno parte tutte della raccolta di Curnoe, e il testo indica da quale città canadese provengono e in quale anno furono acquisite.

L'oggetto ritratto al centro del quadro è una fotografia aerea dell'Ospedale Victoria di London (Ontario), pubblicata nel *The London Free Press* con un sistema di numerazione simile a quello usato dall'artista nella *Veduta dell'Ospedale Victoria, seconda serie (10 febbraio 1969 – 10 marzo 1971)*. Curnoe no sapeva allora dell'esistenza di questa fotografia che Murray Favro, un artista di London, gli regalò dopo che ebbe portato a termine il grande paesaggio (cat. no. 1).

Nella parte superiore sinistra il quadro mostra la mano dell'artista che tiene una fotografia di Michel Chartrand, Presidente del Consiglio Centrale di Montréal affiliato alla Confederazione dei Sindacati Nazionali (C.S.N.) di Montréal. Le due citazioni (trad.): «È la loro universale merda americana» e «Impara con il rullo compressore sulla faccia», sono tolte da una poesia di Bill Bissett, di Vancouver, intitolata *Love of Life th 49th Parallel* scritta nel 1970, pubblicata nella Blewointment Press di Vancouver originalmente, e in seguito in *Nobody owns the Earth* di Bissett, pubblicata da Anansi nel 1971 a Toronto.

La trama sonora è stata registrata sistemando il microfono, nello studio, su una tavola da ping-pong a 3 metri e 5 cm. dalla finestra, dalle 10.40 alle 11.25 del mattino, sabato 6 marzo 1971, e da mezzogiorno alle 12.45, lunedì 8 marzo 1971.

7

Veduta dalla finestra sopra le doppie porte della parete a est, 1971

Acrilico, inchiostro da timbri e carta da parati su legno compensato
cm. 61,6 x cm. 122,6
ESPOSIZIONE: Toronto, The Isaacs Gallery, 25 gennaio – 13 febbraio 1973, *Greg Curnoe* (col titolo, *Veduta dalla finestra sopra le doppie porte della parete a ovest* [e non a *est*]).
COLLEZIONE: LA BANQUE D'ART, CONSEIL DES ARTS DU CANADA, OTTAWA

Il testo stampigliato a destra è di Curnoe (trad.): «Grigio o grigio? Zenith. Il vento si è levato. Il cielo è coperto – grigio pallido con strisce di grigio ancora più pallido. La temperatura fuori è di 20 gradi. Tutte le foglie si muovono sugli alberi, posso sentirle anche se la porta sotto questa finestra è chiusa. Il vento soffia più forte. Il cielo sembra sollevato. Le nuvole più grigie si dirigono rapidamente verso est in uno sfondo grigio più chiaro. Scritto il 15 settembre 1971 – ore 11.55.»
La grafia della parola «GREY» ([trad.]: grigio) è deliberatamente inglese anziché americana.

8

Veduta dalla finestra a destra del centro, sulla parete a nord 24 agosto 1971 – 21 gennaio 1973

Olio, inchiostro da timbri, carta da parati su legno compensato, alto-parlante e nastro sonoro magnetico
cm. 182,9 x cm. 122,0 (sostegno e alto-parlante cm. 48,3)
ESPOSIZIONE: Toronto, The Isaacs Gallery, 25 gennaio – 13 febbraio 1973, *Greg Curnoe.*
COLLEZIONE: CITY SAVINGS AND TRUST COMPANY, VANCOUVER, COLUMBIA BRITANNICA

Nella parte inferiore a sinistra della finestra il testo descrive le circostanze della registrazione della trama sonora (trad.): «La mia macchina da scrivere è sul tavolo sotto la finestra descritta da questo quadro. Martedì 16 gennaio dalle 11.30 del mattino alle 12 e giovedì 18 gennaio dalle 9.30 alle 10 ho dattilografato una descrizione di quel che vedo dalla finestra, con un magnetofono in movimento e il microfono attaccato a un chiodo della struttura della finestra, proprio sopra la macchina da scrivere.»
La vespa di profilo sul lato destro in alto del quadro, come pure una di quelle stampigliate in basso a destra, provengono da un timbro di gomma appartenente al figlio dell'artista Owen. Per gli altri insetti, Curnoe utilizzò un altro stampo di gomma ricavato da un disegno che fece specialmente per il quadro.
Il termometro ritratto a sinistra del quadro, è un regalo che Don e Bernice Vincent fecero a

Curnoe quando si istallò nello studio che occupa oggi. La ditta «Almatex» fabbricava lo smalto giallo chiaro preferito da Curnoe.

La forma blu al centro del quadro in basso è un pezzo di una lampada in vetro blu-oltremarino piazzata sul vetro della finestra. Questo pezzo ha una intensità blu translucida simile a quella della bottiglia di «Bromo» rappresentata nella *Veduta dell'Ospedale Victoria, seconda serie (10 febbraio 1969 – 10 marzo 1971)*. È di un colore che Curnoe pure ama molto.

È così, da questa finestra che Curnoe registra il suo diario su ordinatore.

MOSTRE

(*Mostre personali di Greg Curnoe e mostre scelte di gruppo, queste ultime sono indicate da un asterico.*)

*Toronto, The Garret Gallery, dicembre 1957 (gruppo di nove artisti).

London (Ontario), Richard E. Crouch Branch Library, 3–30 novembre 1961, *Exhibition of things*.

*London (Ontario), Region Gallery, 1962 (?), *Greg Curnoe, Larry Russell*.

*London (Ontario), Region Gallery, marzo 1963, *Greg Curnoe, Brian Dibb*.

*London (Ontario), The McIntosh Memorial Art Gallery, University of Western Ontario, 26 novembre– 19 dicembre 1962, *Mr. Curnoe and Mrs. Cumming*.

Toronto, Gallery Moos, 12–30 settembre 1963, *Greg Curnoe*.

Toronto, David Mirvish Gallery, 17 settembre – 6 ottobre 1964, *Greg Curnoe, «STUFF»*.

*Regina, Norman Mackenzie Art Gallery, 8–31 ottobre 1964, *John Chambers, Greg Curnoe* (con catalogo).

*London (Ontario), The McIntosh Memorial Art Gallery, University of Western Ontario, 9–27 novembre 1964, *Imports and Local Art Work Curnoe Urquhart*.

Vancouver, Art Gallery, 8–27 febbraio 1966, e Edmonton, Art Gallery, 5–31 marzo 1966, Paintings by *Greg Curnoe* (con cataloghi).

Toronto, The Isaacs Gallery, 16 novembre – 5 dicembre 1966, *New Work From Sowesto Greg Curnoe*.

Vancouver, The New Design Gallery, 16 novembre– 5 dicembre 1966, *Recent Collages by Greg Curnoe*.

London (Ontario), 20/20 Gallery, 15 febbraio – 5 marzo 1967, *G. Curnoe's Series*.

Toronto, The Isaacs Gallery, 4–18 aprile 1967, *G. Curnoe's time series*.

*London (Ontario), The McIntosh Memorial Art Gallery, University of Western Ontario, 30 ottobre –

11 novembre 1967, *Chambers and Curnoe Art Exhibit* (con catalogo).

*Regina, Norman Mackenzie Art Gallery, 16 novembre – 17 dicembre 1967, *Statements: 18 Canadian Artists* (con catalogo).

*Parigi, Museo Nazionale d'Arte Moderna, 12 gennaio – 18 febbraio 1968, *Canada. Arte di oggi.* La mostra venne in seguito presentata a Roma, Losanna e Brusselles (con catalogo).

*Edimburgo, College of Art, Festival Internazionale, 18 agosto–7 settembre 1968, *Canada 101* (con catalogo).

*Ottawa, Galleria Nazionale del Canada, 1968–1969, *Cœur de London*. Mostra viaggiante (con catalogo).

Toronto, The Isaacs Gallery, 5–24 febbraio 1969, *Greg Curnoe*.

*London (Ontario), 20/20 Gallery, 22 aprile–11 maggio 1969, *The London Survey*. Mostra di gruppo: Margo Arris, Don Bellamy, Don Bonham, Jack Chambers, Tom Coulter, Greg Curnoe, Kee Dewdney, Paterson Ewen, Murray Favro, R. Fenwick.

*Vancouver, Art Gallery, 13 gennaio – 8 febbraio 1970, *955,000* (con catalogo).

London (Ontario), The McIntosh Memorial Art Gallery, University of Western Ontario, 2–19 aprile 1970, *Greg Curnoe Drawings*.

Toronto, The Isaacs Gallery, 29 aprile – 18 maggio 1970, *Greg Curnoe . . . Collage 1961–70*.

*Montréal, Sir George Williams University e The Saidye Bronfman Centre, 1–17 febbraio 1971, *45° 30′ N–73° 36′ W* (con catalogo).

Toronto, The Isaacs Gallery, 17 marzo – 5 aprile 1971, *Greg Curnoe Views of Victoria Hospital and Wings over the Atlantic*.

Montréal, Waddington Galleries, 16 novembre – 4 dicembre 1971, *Greg Curnoe*.

London (Ontario), The London House, 1–7 febbraio 1972, *Greg Curnoe – Display of Water Colours Measurements and Clockings*.

Toronto, The Isaacs Gallery, 25 gennaio – 13 febbraio 1973, *Greg Curnoe*.

London (Ontario), The Polyglot Gallery, 14 giugno – 5 luglio 1973, *Greg Curnoe – Watercolours and drawings*.

Ottawa, Galleria Nazionale del Canada, 1974–1975, *The Great Canadian Sonnet, Dessins de Greg Curnoe* (mostra itinerante con catalogo).

London (Ontario), The Forest City Art Gallery, 16 novembre – 4 dicembre 1974, *Greg Curnoe Watercolours*.

Toronto, The Isaacs Gallery, 4–21 febbraio 1975, *Greg Curnoe Recent Watercolours*.

London (Ontario), Public Library and Art Gallery, 5–28 settembre 1975, *Some Lettered Works by Greg Curnoe 1961–1969*.

SCRITTI DI GREG CURNOE, IN ORDINE CRONOLOGICO

Senza titolo, 15 gennaio 1961, in *Region*, no. 1 (1961), senza pagina.

Senza titolo, 26 marzo 1961, in *Region*, no. 1 (1961), s.p.

Statement, in *Region*, no. 2 (gennaio 1962), pag. 5.

About Wearing My Dead Grandfather's Glasses, in *Region*, no. 3 (1962), s.p.

Hangover, in *Region*, no. 3 (1962), s.p.

Steering wheel, in *Region*, no. 4 (settembre 1962), s.p.

Confessions of an ex Bicycle Rider, in *Region*, no. 5 (febbraio 1963), pag. 2.

Region = Regionalism, lettera alla redazione, in *The University of Western Ontario Gazette* di London (Ontario), 15 marzo 1963, p. 9.

Senza titolo, in *Region*, no. 6 (1963 ?), s.p.

Prefàzio, catalogo della mostra, *Walt Redinger: Scultore, Ed Zelenak: Scultore, John Boyle: Pittore*, London (Ontario), The McIntosh Memorial Art Gallery, 22 febbraio – 12 marzo 1964.

Selections from 3rd Trip to Montreal, in *Region*, no. 7 (giugno 1964), pagg. 32–34.

Mirrors and Images from the Coke Book, in *Alphabet*, no. 9 (novembre 1964), pagg. 43–47.

Greg Curnoe 1936–, testo in un articolo in collaborazione, *Ten Artists in search of Canadian art,* in *Canadian Art,* Vol. XXIII, no. 1, edizione no. 100 (gennaio 1966), pag. 64.

Not Leftover Art, lettera alla redazione, in *The London Free Press* di London (Ontario), 12 luglio 1966.

Senza titolo, articolo di fondo, in *Region,* no. 8 (estate 1966), s.p.

Radio Journal. Rubrica in *20 Cents Magazine,* vol. I, no. 2 (ottobre 1966), s.p.

A Conversation About Mixed Media from New York City as seen at The University of Western Ontario, November 17 and McMaster University, November 12, 1966, in *20 Cents Magazine,* vol. I, no. 4 (ottobre–novembre 1966), s.p.

Senza titolo, lettera alla redazione, in *20 Cents Magazine,* vol. I, no. 4 (dicembre 1966), s.p.

Radio Journal. Rubrica in *20 Cents Magazine,* vol. I, no. 4 (dicembre 1966), s.p.

Radio Journal. Rubrica in *20 Cents Magazine,* vol. I, no. 5 (gennaio 1967), s.p.

Sensa titolo, lettera alla redazione, in *20 Cents Magazine,* vol. I, no. 5 (gennaio 1967), s.p. (Ristampa di una lettera alla redazione in *The University of Western Ontario Gazette* di London (Ontario), 15 marzo 1963.)

Boyling Point, in *20 Cents Magazine,* vol. I, no. 6 (febbraio 1967), s.p.

Radio Journal. Rubrica in *20 Cents Magazine,* vol. I, no. 6 (febbraio 1967), s.p.

Radio Journal. Rubrica in *20 Cents Magazine,* vol. I, no. 7 (marzo 1967), s.p.

Notes – on the North Wall, in *Region,* no. 9 (primavera 1967), s.p.

Radio Journal. Rubrica in *20 Cents Magazine,* vol. I, no. 8 (aprile 1967), s.p.

Radio Journal. Rubrica in *20 Cents Magazine,* vol. I, no. 9 (maggio 1967), s.p.

Senza titolo, testo nel catalogo dell'esposizione, *Statements: 18 Canadian Artists,* Regina, Norman

Mackenzie Art Gallery, 16 novembre – 17 dicembre 1967, pagg. 38–42.

Radio Journal. Rubrica in *20 Cents Magazine*, vol. II, no. 3 (dicembre (?) 1967), s.p.

Radio Journal, Rubrica in *20 Cents Magazine*, vol. II, no. 4 (marzo (?) 1968), s.p.

Radio Journal. Rubrica in *20 Cents Magazine*, vol. II, no. 5 (giugno (?) 1968), pag. 7.

Radio Journal. Rubrica in *20 Cents Magazine*, vol. II, no. 6 (luglio (?) 1968), pagg. 33–35.

Radio Journal. Rubrica in *20 Cents Magazine*, vol. III, no. 3–4 (maggio 1969), s.p.

N.E. Thing Co. Conference. Articolo nella rubrica *Radio Journal*, in *20 Cents Magazine*, vol. III, no. 5–6 (giugno 1969), s.p.

N.E. Thing Co. Conference (Part Two). Articolo nella rubrica *Radio Journal*, in *20 Cents Magazine*, vol. III, no. 7–8 (ottobre 1969), pag. 20.

Greg Curnoe (from journals written on the C.N.R. on the way to Toronto, 8:55 or so, Wednesday morning, August 13, 1969). Citato (pag. 25) nell'articolo di Mendes Ross: *The Language of the Eyes Windows and Mirrors,* in *Artscanada*, vol. XXVI, no. 5, edizione no. 136/137 (ottobre 1969), pagg. 20–25.

N.E. Thing Co. Conference (Part Three). Articolo nella rubrica *Radio Journal*, in *20 Cents Magazine*, vol. III, no. 9 (novembre 1969), pag. 20.

The Coke Book Continued, in *Alphabet*, no. 17 (dicembre 1969), pag. 20.

Excerpts from Wings Over the Atlantic. Articolo nella rubrica *Radio Journal*, in *20 Cents Magazine*, vol. III, no. 10 (dicembre 1969), pag. 20.

Argomenti proposti de Greg Curnoe e citazioni, in *Greg Curnoe Canada*. Catalogo di Dennis Reid per la X Biennale, San Paolo (Brasile), 1969, pag. 68.

Senza titolo, testo e citazioni in *955,000.* Catalogo redatto da Lucy Lippard (editrice) per Vancouver Art Gallery, 13 gennaio – 8 febbraio 1970.

Radio Journal. Rubrica in *20 Cents Magazine*, vol. I, IV, no. 1 (gennaio 1970), page. 20.

Parker (Harley): *Greg Curnoe's paintings: Moos Gallery, Toronto (settembre 12 – ottobre 2)*, in *Alphabet*, no. 7 (dicembre 1963), pagg. 87–89.

Pratten (Art): *Note from the «Art Editor»* in *20 Cents Magazine*, vol. I, no. 8 (aprile 1967), s.p.

Pringle (Douglas): *The Great Canadian Sonnet*, in *Artscanada*, vol. XXVII, no. 4, edizione no. 146/147 (agosto 1970), pagg. 71–72.

Rabinowitch (Royden): *Nihilists Co-operate*, in *20 Cents Magazine*, vol. I, no. 4 (dicembre 1966), s.p.

Rans (Geoffrey): *A Word (Sotto Voce) About the Region: inside my picket fence in London, Ontario*, in *20 Cents Magazine*, vol. I, no. 5 (gennaio 1967), s.p.

————: 20/20 Gallery: *A Report and a Prediction*, in *20 Cents Magazine*, vol. I, no. 8 (aprile 1967), s.p.

Reaney (James): *Introduzione* al catalogo della mostra, *John Chambers, Greg Curnoe*, Regina, Norman Mackenzie Art Gallery, 8–31 ottobre 1964.

————: *Role of the inscription in painting*, in *Canadian Art*, vol. XXIII, no. 4, edizione no. 103 (ottobre 1966), pagg. 41–45.

Reid (Dennis): *Greg Curnoe Canada*, catalogo della mostra per la X biennale di San Paolo (Brasile), Galleria Nazionale del Canada, Ottawa, 1969.

————: *A Concise History of Canadian Painting*, Oxford University Press, Toronto, 1973.

Robillard (Yves): *L'affaire de la murale de l'aéroport de Dorval*, in *La Presse* di Montréal, 6 aprile 1968.

Rockman (Arnold): *Greg Curnoe at the Gallery Moos, Toronto*, in *Canadian Art*, vol. XXI, no. 1, edizione no. 89 (gennaio–febbraio 1964), pag. 10.

«69»: The object Was to Paint (Print?) 24 Panels, One An Hour for 24 Hours, From 12:00 a.m. Wednesday, December 14th, to 12:00 a.m. Thursday, December 15th. The Panels Were 10 by 10 Sheets of Tin Plate With Lapped Edges, in *20 Cents Magazine*, vol. I, no. 5 (dicembre 1966), s.p.

Ha anche sottoscritto, assieme ad altri, *Open letter to W. O. Twaits, Chairman, Imperial Oil Ltd.* volantino al ciclostile per una manifestazione, Ottawa, 27 maggio 1971.

Notes on Picabia, in *Artscanada,* vol. XVIII, no. 4, edizione no. 158/159 (agosto–settembre 1971), pagg. 70–71.

(Con Bozak [Bob]): *Artists dispute Fanshawe College Statement,* lettera alla redazione in *The London Free Press* di London (Ontario), 2 novembre 1971.

Art Purchase, lettera alla redazione, *The London Free Press* di London (Ontario), 4 gennaio 1972.

Critica di *The Projector* di M. Vaughn-James (Toronto: 1971), in *The Canadian Forum,* vol. LII, no. 617 (giugno 1972), pagg. 40–41.

(Con Théberge [Pierre]): *For Dan Patterson and Arthème St. Germain/Pour Dan Patterson et Arthème St-Germain.* Manifesto dell'Associazione per la documentazione degli aspetti negletti della cultura nel Canada. Foglietto in ciclostile, 8 agosto 1972. Pubblicato in *La Revue de l'Association pour la documentation des Aspects Négligés de la Culture au Canada,* t. 1, no. 1, pag. 1.

From the Blue Book/Journals, in *Open Letter,* Seconda Serie, no. 4 (primavera 1973), pagg. 94-108.

Notebook Greg Curnoe, in *Proof Only,* vol. I, no. 1 (15 novembre 1973), pagg. 2–3.

Canadian Painters, lettera alla redazione. in *The Globe and Mail* di Toronto, 26 novembre 1973.

David McFadden in *The Great Canadian Sonnet Dessins de Greg Curnoe,* catalogo della mostra, Ottawa, Galleria Nazionale del Canada, 1974, s.p.

(Con Bergeron [Léandre]): *A Bi-Focus on Barry Lord: The History of Painting in Canada* in *Books in Canada,* t. 3, no. 8 (dicembre 1974), pagg. 20, 36–38.

The Dilemma of Provincialism A History of Canadian Painting (critica da Reid, Dennis: A Concise History of Canadian Painting, Toronto 1973) in *The Canadian Forum,* t. 54, no. 648 (febbraio 1975), pagg. 30–32.

Introduction in *Some Lettered Works by Greg
Curnoe 1961-1969,* catalogo della mostra, London
(Ontario), Public Library and Art Gallery, 5–28
settembre 1975

BIBLIOGRAFIA SCELTA

An artistics affront to Americans, articolo di fondo,
in *The London Free Press* di London (Ontario), 2
aprile 1968, pag. 6.

Bisset (Bill): *Nobody owns th earth,* Anansi, Toronto, 1971.

Bodolai (Joe): *Borderlines in Art and Experience* in
Artscanada, t. XXXI, no. 1, edizione no. 188/189
(primavera 1974), pagg. 65–81.

Boyle (John B.): *Continental Refusal/Refus Continental,* in *20 Cents Magazine,* vol. IV, no. 4
(aprile 1970), s.p.

Chandler (John, Noel): *More Words on Curnoe's
Wordly World,* in *Artscanada,* vol. XXVI, no. 2,
edizione no. 130/131 (aprile 1969), pagg. 3–8.

————: *Painting «From Life»: Greg Curnoe at
the Isaacs Gallery Ltd.,* in *Artscanada,* vol.
XXVIII, no. 3, edizione no. 156–157 (giugno–luglio
1961), pag. 75.

————: *sources are resources: Greg Curnoe's objects, objectives and objection,* in *Artscanada,*
vol. XXX, no. 1, edizione no. 176/177 (febbraio-
marzo 1973), pag. 69.

Cobb (David): *A man of Involvement,* in *Toronto
Daily Star* di Toronto, 14 settembre 1963, pag. 29.

Coleman (Victor): *Knowing the surface,* in *Artscanada,* vol. XXIX, no. 1, edizione no. 164/165 (febbraio–marzo 1972), pagg. 71–72.

Crawford (Lenore): *Spoofs Reveal Artist, Odd Objects Exhibit Startles Art Lovers,* in *The London
Free Press* di London (Ontario), 4 novembre 1961.

————: *G. Curnoe and K. T. Cumming at the
McIntosh Memorial Art Gallery, University of*

Western Ontario, London, in *Canadian Art,* vol. XX, no. 2, edizione no. 84 (marzo–aprile 1963), pagg. 86, 87

————: *Londoners step up invasion of Montreal Art Galleries,* in *The London Free Press* di London (Ontario), 4 aprile 1964.

————: *Urquhart, Curnoe exhibit a mixture of color, vitality, humor,* in *The London Free Press* di London (Ontario), 14 novembre 1964, pag. 21.

————: *Artist Curnoe more «Involved» than ever,* in *The London Free Press* di London (Ontario), 3 dicembre 1966.

————: *«The Spasms»,* in *The London Free Press* di London (Ontario), 3 febbraio 1968, pag. 35.

————: *«Before storm»,* in *The London Free Press* di London (Ontario), 30 marzo 1968.

————: *Curnoe art dominates new show,* in *The London Free Press* di London (Ontario), 21 luglio 1970.

————: *Curnoe displays art in Toronto,* in *The London Free Press* di London (Ontario), 20 marzo 1971.

————: *Canada buys Curnoe work,* in *The London Free Press* di London (Ontario), 14 agosto 1971.

————: *Curnoe «on the spot» water-colors show «first» for old hotel,* in *The London Free Press* di London (Ontario), 2 febbraio 1972.

————: *Curnoe reveals superb new talent,* in *The London Free Press* di London (Ontario), 25 giugno 1973.

Curnoe – A File Interview, in *File,* vol. II, no. 1–2 (aprile-maggio 1973), pagg. 46, 47 e 61.

Curnoe At The Front in *Georgia Straight,* di Vancouver, 6–13 giugno 1974.

Dault (Gary, Michael): *Heart of London,* in *Arts-canada,* vol. XXV, no. 4, edizione no. 122/123 (ottobre–novembre 1968), pag. 43.

————: *Greg Curnoe's love of bicycles expressed in beautiful paintings,* in *The Toronto Star* di Toronto, 7 febbraio 1975.

Davis (Rae): *The Life of death in London,* in *Canadian Art,* vol. XXIII, no. 3, edizione no. 102 (luglio 1966), pagg. 20–25, 50–51.

Hale (Barry): *Stick around and work with what's around you,* in *Saturday Night,* vol. LXXXV, no. 1, edizione no. 3499 (gennaio 1970), pagg. 25–29.

Harris (Marjorie): *Nihilist Spasm Band,* in *Artscanada,* vol. XXV, no. 2, edizione no. 118–119 (giugno 1968), pagg. 6–47.

Kidd (Bruce): *Bruce Kidd interviews Greg Curnoe,* in *The Canadian Forum,* vol. LIII, no. 631 (agosto 1973), pagg. 22–30.

Lord (Barry): *Painters Became Politically Aware in '68,* in *Kitchener-Waterloo Record* di Kitchener-Waterloo (Ontario), 28 dicembre 1968.

————:*What London, Ontario has that everywhere else needs,* in *Art in America,* vol. LVII, no. 5 (settembre–ottobre 1969), pagg. 103–105.

————:*The History of Painting in Canada, Toward a People's Art,* N.C. Press, Toronto 1974.

McFadden (David): *The Great Canadian Sonnet,* illustrazioni di Greg Curnoe, Coach House, Toronto, 1970.

————: *Au sujet de Greg Curnoe, artiste* in *The Great Canadian Sonnet Dessins de Greg Curnoe,* catalogo della mostra, Ottawa, Galleria Nazionale del Canada, 1974.

McKenzie (Robert C.): *Beaver kosmos: A Narrowminded Review,* in *20 Cents Magazine,* vol. I, no. 8 (aprile 1967), s.p.

————: *Greg Curnoe's Connexions,* in *20 Cents Magazine,* vol. IV, no. 3 (marzo 1970), s.p.

McPherson (Huso): *Greg Curnoe's Shorthand,* in *20 Cents Magazine,* vol. I, no. 6 (febbraio 1967), s.p.

Mendes (Ross): *The Language of the eyes – Windows and Mirrors,* in *Artscanada,* vol. XXVI, no. 5, edizione no. 136/137 (ottobre 1969), pagg. 20–25.

Oille (Jennifer): *Greg Curnoe at the Isaacs Gallery* in *Only Paper Today,* t. 2, no. 6, marzo 1975, pag. 2.

The Mothers of Invention – Ron Bohman and Greg Curnoe in Conversation. Articolo nella rubrica *Radio Journal,* in *20 Cents Magazine,* vol. IV, no. 2 (febbraio 1970), s.p.

Greg Curnoe's Radio Journal. Rubrica in *20 Cents Magazine,* vol. IV, no. 3 (marzo 1970), s.p.

Amendments to Continental Refusal/Refus Continental, in *20 Cents Magazine,* vol. IV, no. 4 (aprile 1970), s.p.

Greg Curnoe's Radio Journal. Rubrica in *20 Cents Magazine,* vol. IV, no. 4 (aprile 1970), s.p.

Greg Curnoe's Radio Journal. Rubrica in *20 Cents Magazine,* vol. IV, no. 5–6 (giugno 1970), s.p.

Prefàzio. Catalogo della mostra, *Inventions and Perpetual Motion Machines,* London (Ontario), 20/20 Gallery, 2–21 giugno 1970.

Greg Curnoe's Radio Journal. Rubrica in *20 Cents Magazine,* vol. IV, no. 7 (settembre 1970), pag. 20.

Curnoe on London, in *The London Free Press* di London (Ontario), 17 ottobre 1970.

The most beautiful book in the world (critica dell' *Economic Atlas of Ontario, Toronto,* 1970), in *Artscanada,* vol. XXVII, no. 6, edizione no. 150/151 (dicembre 1970 – gennaio 1971), pagg. 64–65.

(In collaborazione con McFadden [David]): *The Great Canadian Sonnet,* Coach House, Toronto, 1970. Illustrazioni di Greg Curnoe.

In collaborazione, *Snore Comix, Bright Things,* Coach House, Toronto, 1970.

Senza titolo, testi di Greg Curnoe pagg. 7 e 76, in *The cosmic chef an evening of concrete,* Nichol, B. P. (editore), Ottawa: Oberon, 1970.

Senza titolo, testo in 45° 30′ N – 73° 36′ W. Catalogo dell'esposizione di Gary Coward, Bill Vazan, Arthur Bardo e Zoe Notkin (editore), Montréal, università Sir George William e The Saidye Bronfman Centre, 1–17 febbraio 1971.

Kasabonika – Simmons – Thomas – Curry – Dic – St. Germain – Patterson – Stansell – Laithwaite, ecc. Relazione dattilografata sull'arte popolare per il Museo Nazionale dell'Uomo, Ottawa, ottobre 1970 – marzo 1971.

Théberge (Pierre): *Confessions of a Nihilist Spasm Band Addict,* in *Artscanada,* vol. XXVI, no. 6, edizione no. 138/139 (dicembre 1969), pagg. 66–68.

———: *Soixante dessins de Greg Curnoe pour The Great Canadian Sonnet de David McFadden «. . . beau(x) . . . comme la rencontre fortuite sur une table de dissection d'une machine à coudre et d'un parapluie!»* (*Lautréamont*) in *The Great Canadian Sonnet Dessins de Greg Curnoe,* catalogo della mostra, Ottawa, Galleria Nazionale del Canada, 1974.

Thompson (David): *A Canadian scene: 3,* in *Studio International,* vol. CLXXVI, no. 906 (dicembre 1968), pagg. 241–245.

Wallace (Helen): *Remove objectionable Curnoe airport art,* in *The London Free Press* di London (Ontario), 28 marzo 1968, pag. 31.

———: *Anti-American work by Curnoe removed from Dorval Airport Mural,* in *The London Free Press* di London (Ontario), 29 marzo 1968, pagg. 1, 10.

———: *While controversy rages,* in *The London Free Press* di London (Ontario), 30 marzo 1968.

The Weekly Interview, Greg Curnoe (*Part 1*), in *The London Weekly* di London (Ontario), 16 luglio

The Weekly Interview, Greg Curnoe (*Part II*), in *The London Weekly* di London (Ontario), 23 luglio 1968.

Woodman (Ross): *Greg Curnoe.* Introduzione su foglietto in ciclostile per la mostra *Greg Curnoe Series* London (Ontario), 20/20 Gallery, 15 febbraio – 5 marzo 1967.

———: *London (Ont.): a new regionalism,* in *Artscanada,* vol. XXIV, no. 8–9, edizione no. 111/112 (agosto–settembre 1967), inserto, s.p.

———: *London: regional liberation front,* in *The Globe and Mail* di Toronto, 13 dicembre 1969.

1

0.SHADOW OCCURS AT 4.30 OR SO E.S.T.

1.FLASH OF A WINDSHEILD FEB.27-1969.5.P.M.

2.HEADLIGHTS GO PAST HOSPITAL MAR.20-12.P.M.

3.OWEN MARKS THE PANEL HERE WITH A BLACK FELT MARK
  ING PEN & I GET MAD MAR.25-11.45.A.M.

4.A GROUP OF PEOPLE WALKING IN FRONT OF BLACKWOOD
  LODGE MAR.25-5 TO 2.P.M.

5.A DROP OF WATER RUNNING DOWN THE OUTSIDE OF THE
  CENTREPRIGHT WINDOW PANE MAR.24-12.45.P.M.

6.A XXXXX HUGE ROUND PUFF OF SMOKE MAY 15.-9.P.M.

7.JACK WAS HERE JULY 15-APPROX.

8.DUMP TRUCK ON ROAD-MOVING EAST AT LEFT CHIMNEY 1
  NOV.28-10 TO 2.P.M.

9.WINDOW SHINY FEB.22-1970.3.P.M.

10.TWO SUN REFLECTIONS-CONSTANT MAR.19-AFTERNOON.

11.WHISP OF BLACK SMOKE MOVING WEST MAR.19-AFTERNOO
  N.

12.LIGHT AT WEST END OF BLACKWOOD LODGE MAR.20-4.30
  P.M.

13.LIGHT BELOW & LEFT OF LARGE MIDDLE UPPER WINDOW
  MAR.20-10.A.M.

14.DOT OF LIGHT MAR.23-NOON.

15.A LOT OF BLACK SMOKE FROM CITIES HEATING MAR.25-
  3.55.P.M.

16. A FLASH APR.7-NO TIME.

17. A CAR GOES OUT OF HOSPITAL PARKING LOT FROM EAST
    -TURNS ONTO COLBORNE STREET-GOES NORTH APR.9-11.
    15.P.M.

18. DAD IN OBSERVATION ROOM WAVING-SOMETIME IN APR.

19. FLUTTERING WINGS MAY 5-5 AFTER 10.A.M.

20. TWO VERY BRIGHT BLUISH LIGHTS-ONE ABOVE THE OTHE
    R MAY 8-5 TO 9.P.M.

21. THE RAIN HIT THE OLD POST OFFICE & FLAG BEFORE H
    ERE NO DATE OR TIME-AFTERNOON.

22. BIRDS ON FIELD JUNE 10-A QUARTER AFTER 2.P.M.

23. NOTICED WHERE PAINT WAS CHIPPED OFF CEILING JUNE
    12-2.50.P.M.

24. AMERICAN B58A HUSTLER SHOT DOWN BY CANADIAN SMAL
    L ARMS FIRE JUNE 18.-12.30.P.M.

25. SMALLISH DARK CLOUD DIRECTLY OVER THE TWO CHIMNE
    KYS & SMOKE GOING STRAIGHT UP OUT OF CHIMNEY ON
    THE RIGHT JULY 30-7.30.P.M.

26. FIRST RECORDING MADE WITH MICROPHONE ON BLUE PIC
    KET FENCE-ERASED JULY

27. SECOND RECORDING MADE WITH MICROPHONE ON TREE ST
    UMP-ERASED AUG.4.

28. THIRD RECORDING MADE WITH MICROPHONE ON BLUE PIC
    KET FENCE-WITH JIMMY & GLEN AUG.9-8.P.M.TO 9.P.M

29. FOURTH RECORDING MADE WITH MICROPHONE ON BLUE PI
    CKET FENCE AUG.16-10.25.TO 11.25.P.M.

30.CAR TRACKS IN THE GRASS MADE BY OUR AUSTIN 1100
AUG.20--AFTERNOON

31.FIFTH RECORDING MADE WITH MICROPHONE ON WEST SID
E OF SECOND FROM WEST WALL NORTH WINDOW AUG.23--
5.30 TO 5.35.A.M.

32.LOTS OF BLACK SMOKE-A FIRE AUG.24--20 AFTER 11.P
.M.

XXXXXXXXXXXXXXXXXXXXXXXXXXXXXXXXXXXXXXXXXXXXXXXXXXX
XXX

33.THREE BIRDS WITH WHITE BREASTS AUG.26--10.30.A.M

34.THREE BUTTERFLYS AUG.26--10 AFTER 2.P.M.

35.LARGE BUG FLIES PAST WINDOW SEPT.2--20 TO 4.P.M.

36.I NOTICE THAT THE WHITE PAINT DRIP IS RIGHT ON T
HE HOSPITAL & THE ROW OF EVERGREENS SEPT.20--NO
TIME.

37.LOOKING OUT THE WINDOW AT HERE AFTER ARCHIES PHO
NE CALL SEPT.--25 AFTER 5.P.M.

38.TOLD THAT C.B.WAS HERE SEPT.--NO SPECIFIC DATE O
R TIME.

39.2 RED LIGHTS SEPT.9--12.20.A.M.

40." " "   " "   "   " .

41.LIGHT JUST ABOVE THE EAST END OF THE APARTMENT B
UILDING-IN THE TREES SEPT.9--12.22.A.M.

42.LIGHT ABOVE RED BUILDING ON TOWER SEPT.9--12.23.
A.M.

43. LOWER FLOOR LIT UP SEPT.9--12.25.A.M.

44. LIGHT WINKING SEPT.9--12.45.A.M.

45. TWO TRACTORS & A VOLKSWAGEN PARKED ON THE SHADE
SEPT.10--QUARTER TO 12.A.M.

46. GRASS MOWED BEFORE NOON SEPT.10--NO SPECIFIC TIM
E.

47. BLACK SMOKE SEPT.11--25 AFTER 12.P.M.

48. WHITE CLOUD BEHIND HANGING BROMO BOTTLE SEPT.11-
-20 TO 4.P.M.

49. NOTICED INSECTS IN THE BROMO BOTTLE SEPT.11--20
TO 4.P.M.

50. TWO BUTTERFLYS FLY PAST SEPT.11--QUARTER TO 4.P.
M.

51. NOTICED SEARCHLIGHTS-THOUGHT OF HAL-FAIRGROUNDS
SEPT.11--9.30.P.M.

52. BLUE JAY FLIES TO TREE BELOW POLE OCT.1--10 TO 1
2.A.M.

53. SHEILA POINTS OUT THE ROOM WHERE SHE HAD GALEN O
CT.8--10.30.P.M.

54. FLASHING LIGHT-A SIREN OCT.8--10 TO 12.P.M.

55. THIS TREE HAS TURNED BRIGHT YELLOW-ORANGE OCT.9-
-5 TO 11.A.M.

56. BRANCHES WAVING OCT.8--1.30.P.M.

57. DARK"C"SHAPED CLOUD OCT.8--20 TO 6.P.M.

58.PATH OF A FALLING DROP OF WATER OCT.12--3.P.M.

59.GREY AMERICAN CAR PARKED ON ROAD OCT.13--10 TO 1
2.A.M.

60.LARGE CRANE MOVING TO THE RIGHT OCT.20--10.30.A.
M.

61.LIGHT BLUE AMERICAN CAR GOING WEST ON ROAD SLOWL
Y OCT.20--25 TO 11.A.M.

62.CRANE OCT.23--11.15.A.M.

63.SELWYN ON THE PHONE OCT.26--9.39.P.M.

64.MARY SIGNALS WITH MIRROR OCT.27--20 TO 11.A.M.

XXX

65.RED LIGHT NOV.4--5.30.P.M.

66.WHISP OF BLACK SMOKE NOV.4--5.30.P.M.

67.REFLECTION OF JEAN BELIVEAU HOCKEY GAME IN WINDO
W NOV.4--5.32.P.M.

68.MOTORCYCLE WITH HEADLIGHT ON GOING FAST ON ROAD
NOV.4--5.35.P.M.

69.CAR LIGHTS FLASHING NOV.4--11.P.M.

70.LIGHT GOES OUT NOV.4--11.05.P.M.

71.LIGHT GOES OFF NO TIME OR DATE

72.LIGHT FLICKERS NOV.9--12.30.A.M.

73.BRIGHT BLUISH STREET LIGHT NOV.9--12.35.A.M.

74. STEAM SHOVEL DIGGING NOV.9--4.10.P.M.

75. LEAF FALLS NOV.10--11.20.P.M.

76. MOTORCYCLE PARKED NOV.11--12.20.P.M.

77. BLACK SMOKE BLOWS WEST NOV.11--12.05.P.M.

78. IRENE SIGNALLS WITH FLASHLIGHT & ROOM LIGHT FROM
SELWYNS ROOM NOV.11--7.P.M.

79. RED SIGN NOV.12--10.30.P.M.

80. 63 SHOULD BE HERE.

81. SHEILA POINTS OUT REFLECTIONS FROM THE SUN ON TH
E HOSPITAL WINDOWS NOV.13--5 TO 5.P.M.

82. CAR COES AROUND CORNER & FAST-SEEN THROUGH FALLI
NG SNOW NOV.14--A QUARTER TO 11.P.M.

83. I NOTICE MANHOLE COVER FOR THE FIRST TIME NOV.15
--20 TO 12.A.M.

84. STEAM SHOVEL AT SOUTHWEST CORNER OF APARTMENT BU
ILDING NOV.23--5 AFTER 10.P.M.

85. SNOW IN GROOVE NOV.23--5 AFTER 10.A.M.

86. PILES OF DIRTY SNOW NOV.30--2.20.P.M.

87. WHITE SPIRE NOV.30--2.25.P.M.

88. STEAM RISING FROM RED BRICK BUILDING DEC.10--11.
15.P.M.

89. CRANE DEC.10--11.30.A.M.

90. BRIGHT LIGHT AT REAR OF APARTMENT DEC.15--4.30.P
.M.

91.PILES OF DIRTY SNOW DEC.15--4.30.P.M.

92.DOREEN TELLS ME SHE WAS HERE DEC.23--15 TO 12.A.
M.

93.SMOKE DEC.28--2.P.M.

94.SAM IN BACKYARD XX JAN.2.1971--2.15.P.M.

95.THREE BIRDS FLY TO HERE JAN.4--11.30.A.M.

96. "   "   "   "   "   " "   "   " .

97.LIGHT BULB REFLECTED IN WINDOW JAN.5--3.30.P.M.

98.A LOT OF STEAM JAN.22--20 TO 10.A.M.

99.ORANGE TRUCK-MOUNTED CRANE PARKED JAN.23--2.30.P
.M.

100.DUMP TRUCK DUMPING SNOW JAN.23--2.30.P.M.

101.LTC BUS GOING WEST-GOES BEHIND BLACKWOOD LODGE
JAN.23--2.35.P.M.

102.BULLDOZER MOVING SNOW FEB.12--2.P.M.

103.DIRTY SNOW PILED HIGHER THAN IVE EVER SEEN OUT
BACK FEB.12--2.P.M.

104.GALEN BREAKS OFF HIS FRONT TOOTH FEB.12--AROUND
4.P.M.

105.I FALL DOWN ON THE ICE AT TECUMSEH CARRYING GAL
EN & HE HITS HIS HEAD FEB.13--AROUND 7.30.P.M.

106.STEAM FEB.14--20 TO 5.P.M.

XX

107.BIRD FLYING NORTH FEB.14.--18 TO 5.P.M.

108.ORANGE CRANE PARKED FEB.14.--18 TO 5.P.M.

109.WHITE VAN GOES EAST FEB.17.--20 TO 4.P.M.

110.SNOW SCRAPED AWAY-EARTH SHOWING THROUGH-IN GROO
VE FEB.17.--18 TO 4.P.M.

111.STEAM HANGING IN THE AIR FEB.17.--15 TO 4.P.M.

XXXXXXXXXXXXXX

112.A GUY SHOVELLING SNOW IN THE GROOVE FEB.18.--1
30.P.M.

113.A HAWK FEB.18.--1.35.P.M.

114.SOMEONE WALKING EAST FEB.18.--1.40.P.M.

115.ORANGE VAN PARKED FEB.18.--1.45.P.M.

116.BARELY VISIBLE DARK SMOKE COMING FROM LEFT CHI
MNEY FEB.18.--15 AFTER 4.P.M.

117.A BIG CRANE PARKED FEB.25.--5.15.P.M.

118.LISTENING TO SYRINX TN 2 FEB.26.--5 TO 3.P.M.

119.TOP OF NEW BUILDING IS RED MAR.6.--15 TO 12.P.
M.

120.REDDISH CAST ON BUILDING MAR.6.--10 TO 12.P.M.

VIEW OF VICTORIA HOSPITAL-SECOND SERIES-XXXXXXXXXX
FEB.10.1969 TO MAR.10.1971 GREG CURNOE LONDON ONT

2

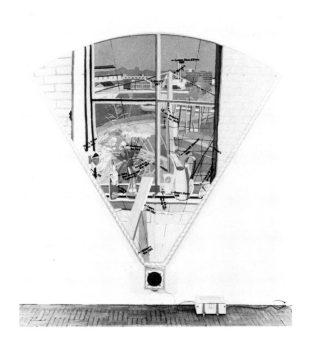

5

6

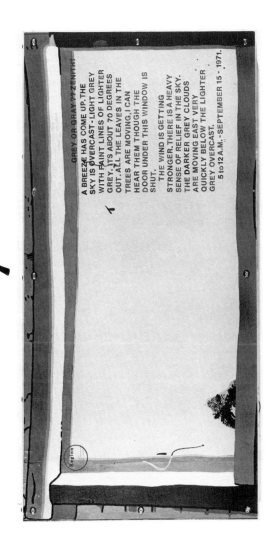

GREY OR GRAY?? ZENITH!

A BREEZE HAS COME UP. THE
SKY IS OVERCAST - LIGHT GREY
WITH FAINT LINES OF LIGHTER
GREY. ITS ABOUT 70 DEGREES
OUT. ALL THE LEAVES IN THE
TREES ARE MOVING, I CAN
HEAR THEM THOUGH THE
DOOR UNDER THIS WINDOW IS
SHUT.

THE WIND IS GETTING
STRONGER. THERE IS A HEAVY
SENSE OF RELIEF IN THE SKY.
THE DARKER GREY CLOUDS
ARE MOVING EAST VERY
QUICKLY BELOW THE LIGHTER
GREY OVERCAST.

5 to 12 A.M. - SEPTEMBER 15 - 1971.

CANADA

GREG CURNOE

XXXVIIe Exposition biennale internationale
d'art, Venise, 1976

Organisée par la Galerie nationale du Canada,
Ottawa
Un des Musées nationaux du Canada

PRÊTEURS

The Alumni Association of the University of
Western Ontario, London, Ontario

L'artiste, par l'entremise de The Isaacs Gallery,
Toronto

La Banque d'art, Conseil des arts du Canada,
Ottawa

City Savings and Trust Company, Vancouver

M. E. J. Escaf, Lambeth, Ontario

Ontario Heritage Foundation, Toronto

Dr M. Robinson, London, Ontario

PRÉFACE

C'est la douzième participation du Canada à la Biennale de Venise. Un commissaire québécois, M. Pierre Théberge, administrateur de la conservation à la Galerie nationale du Canada, a choisi de présenter l'œuvre d'un peintre ontarien, Greg Curnoe, et a écrit, à son sujet, des pages élogieuses dans ce catalogue. En organisant cette exposition nous sommes redevables aux prêteurs, dont certains habitent jusqu'en Colombie-Britannique, de nous avoir permis de montrer à Venise les œuvres les plus colorées et les plus puissantes de Curnoe. Comme toujours, lors d'expositions à l'étranger, la Galerie nationale doit beaucoup à la collaboration de la division des affaires culturelles du ministère canadien des Affaires extérieures et, tout particulièrement, elle est reconnaissante de l'aide fournie par notre ambassade de Rome. Elle remercie également l'ambassade d'Italie à Ottawa de son concours.

La directrice
de la Galerie nationale du Canada
Jean Sutherland Boggs

Figure I

INTRODUCTION

Greg Curnoe habite London (Ontario) où il est né en 1936. C'est une ville de 225 000 habitants, située dans le sud-ouest de la province, où il existe un milieu artistique très actif.

Non seulement peintre mais aussi écrivain Curnoe tient, concurremment depuis des années, plusieurs journaux personnels[1] où il consigne de façon suivie des observations sur sa vie quotidienne. Il a aussi fondé et dirigé, de 1961 à 1967, la revue *Region* de London et a collaboré régulièrement, de 1966 à 1970, à la revue *20 Cents Magazine,* publiée également dans cette ville.

Greg Curnoe a aussi fait des films[2].

Collectionneur acharné, il a accumulé entre autres, des bouteilles de liqueurs douces fabriquées par des petites entreprises de tous les coins du Canada[3], des cartes géographiques du pays, des bicyclettes et des revues de cyclisme, des livres sur les dirigeables et des «Big Little Books»[4], des instruments topographiques et une grande quantité de disques de musique folklorique populaire contemporaine.

Greg Curnoe est en plus coureur cycliste amateur[5].

Il s'intéresse passionnément à la culture populaire dans toutes ses manifestations en tant que membre actif de l'Association pour la documentation des aspects négligés de la culture au Canada dont il fut, en 1972, le co-fondateur, et il a amassé une importante collection de diapositives sur l'art populaire[6].

Il est aussi membre d'une coopérative d'alimentation et d'une coopérative d'artistes fondée en décembre 1973, la Forest City Art Gallery de London. Il fut aussi l'un des fondateurs de trois autres coopératives, la première à Toronto, The Garrett Gallery (1957–1959) et les deux autres à London, la Region Gallery (1961–1963) et la 20/20 Gallery (1966–1970).

Actuellement Curnoe est le porte-parole de l'Ontario à la CAR (Canadian Artists Representation), une association nationale d'artistes canadiens. Il est l'un des présidents et l'un des membres fondateurs du Parti nihiliste de London[7]. Ce parti consacre toutes ses ressources à l'organisation d'un pique-nique, et d'un banquet annuels pour ses membres. Il a été nommé le 1er juillet 1975 artiste résident pour un an à l'University of Western Ontario, à London.

Il joue du «kazoo» avec le Nihilist Spasm Band[8], un orchestre bruitiste qui, depuis 1965, s'est produit plus ou moins régulièrement, les lundis soir, dans les tavernes de London et qui actuellement joue à la Forest City Art Gallery.

C'est un régionaliste convaincu et un porte-parole militant de l'anti-américanisme systématique. C'est à ce titre qu'il est le co-auteur avec John Boyle, peintre de St Catharines (Ontario), du manifeste *Refus continental,* publié en 1969[9].

Greg Curnoe est marié, et il a trois enfants.

Toute son œuvre est autobiographique. Il a choisi délibérément de circonscrire le champ de son activité à sa région, London, Ontario, et c'est en elle qu'il puise généralement ses thèmes. Pour lui il n'y a de culture possible qui si elle est régionale, et il n'y a d'art possible que s'il a sa source immédiate dans l'expérience quotidienne. Sa peinture est spontanée, sans programme systématique, et s'y retrouve tout ce qui retient, pour une raison ou pour une autre, son attention momentanée. Greg Curnoe se considère comme un artisan, un bricoleur, un observateur tout à fait subjectif de la réalité. Un seul principe le motive: le plaisir qu'il trouve à faire ce qu'il fait. Greg Curnoe veut que son art soit partie intégrante de sa vie, et qu'il reflète autant que possible tout ce qui l'intéresse[10].

Les tableaux qui sont présentés dans cette exposition correspondent aux huit fenêtres réparties sur trois des quatre murs de l'atelier qu'il occupe depuis 1968 (fig. I). Ces œuvres s'ajoutent à une longue série, commencée en 1961, décrivant ce qu'il voyait des fenêtres des deux ateliers précédents; elles reflètent une attitude commune, celle de l'examen bienveillant de la réalité telle que cadrée par le hasard des constructions[11].

NOTES

1.   La maison d'édition Coach House Press de Toronto prépare une édition facsimilée de cinq volumes de l'un de ces journaux, *The Blue Book,* écrit d'août 1964 à mars 1967. Curnoe continue d'ailleurs cette série. L'édition d'un autre journal, *The Coke Book,* est en préparation chez Alphabet Press à London, Ontario. Curnoe tient, concurremment, aussi un «journal sonore» sur cassettes. Il fit son premier enregistrement le 19 mars 1968 lors d'un voyage en automobile, de London à Montréal, avec le poète Robert Fones.

2.   Il a fait deux films. Le premier, *Sowesto* (1947–1969), un film muet de 16 mm, en couleurs, de 30 minutes. Le second, *Connexions* (1969–1970), un film sonore de 16 mm, en couleurs, de 15 minutes.

3.   Ces bouteilles sont, entre autres, importantes pour Curnoe car elles démontrent l'existence de

cultures régionales au Canada. La forme des bouteilles, le dessin des marques de commerce varient
d'une région à l'autre. Même la saveur, à l'intérieur d'une même recette le «cream soda» ou la
«bière d'épinette» par exemple, est différente
selon la marque et le lieu d'origine, ce qui indique
des préférences régionales tout à fait précises.
4. Livres illustrés pour enfants, publiés princi-
palement pendant les années quarante.

Curnoe a illustré de cent quatre-vingt-quatorze
dessins le livre de David McFadden, *The Great
Canadian Sonnet,* publié en deux volumes, en
1970, selon le principe et le format des «Big
Little Books». La conception caractéristique de
ce genre d'ouvrage, illustrations entourées d'un
cadre noir et accompagnées d'une légende per-
mettait aux enfants de «lire» le livre indépen-
damment du texte.
5. Si à l'automne 1973, il a gagné un trophée du
club cycliste, les «London Centennial Wheelers»,
ce n'est pas comme bon cycliste mais pour son
assiduité aux courses hebdomadaires du club. Il
a d'autre part, conçu et fait fabrique en 1975, le
maillot des membres du club.

En 1972, avant de terminer ses tableaux des
vues des huit fenêtres de son présent atelier de
la rue Weston, Curnoe a fait une série de
«portraits» de deux de ses bicyclettes, la «CCM
1951» et la «Zeus». Ils sont à l'acrylique sur du
contre-plaqué découpé selon le contour de la
machine. En 1973, il a entrepris une autre série
de «portraits» de toutes ses bicyclettes, toujours
de grandeur nature, mais cette fois à l'aquarelle
sur du papier de format rectangulaire; concurremment il a aussi commencé la même année une

troisième série de «portraits», des roues de bicyclettes sur du papier de format carré.

6.   Cette association, selon son manifeste, a pour but de «brouiller la frontière artificielle entre les «beaux»−arts et la culture». Elle se propose de publier, un jour, les documents photographiques qu'elle accumule. Pierre Théberge en est le co-fondateur et le co-président. L'Association a présenté, du 6 décembre 1974 au 2 janvier 1975 plus de six cents diapositives d'objets «négligés» à la Public Library and Art Museum de London, en Ontario et a publié le premier numéro de sa revue à cette occasion.

7.   Le mot NO ([trad.]: non) est le seul programme du Parti Nihiliste. Tous les membres en sont simultanément présidents.

8.   Le «kazoo» est un instrument de musique à bouche.

Le Nihilist Spasm Band a enregistré en 1968 un disque pour Allied Record Corporation de Toronto. Cet orchestre a aussi joué à Paris pendant la VIe Biennale des jeunes et à l'Institute of Contemporary Art de Londres, en octobre 1969. Il comptait alors, outre Curnoe, six autres musiciens: John B. Boyle, William A. Exley, Murray Favro, Archie Leitch, Hugh McIntyre et Art Pratten. Tous les instruments, à l'exception des tambours, sont des inventions des membres de l'orchestre.

9.   Le titre du manifeste paraphrase celui de Paul-Émile Borduas, le *Refus global,* publié en août 1948.

Cette attitude lui a d'ailleurs causé certains ennuis lorsqu'elle s'est exprimée dans son œuvre. En 1968, par exemple, une murale pour l'aéroport international de Montréal à Dorval, commandée par le ministère des Transports du Canada, ne fut jamais installée vu son anti-américanisme. L'œuvre se trouve présentement en dépôt à la Galerie nationale du Canada, à Ottawa. Un autre projet de murale, financé par une compagnie de tabac, qui devait être peinte sur un édifice de Toronto, fut refusé pour les mêmes raisons. Curnoe s'interdit d'exposer aux États-Unis.

10.   «Bruce Kidd: As-tu l'intention de préserver chaque instant de ta vie?

Greg Curnoe: D'abord, je ne préserve pas chaque instant je ne pourrais pas. Cela voudrait dire que toutes mes heures de veille seraient occupées à cette préservation. Je fais seulement ce qui m'intéresse.» Texte traduit de l'anglais, *Bruce Kidd interviews Greg Curnoe,* dans *The Canadian Forum,* t. LIII, n° 631, août 1973, p. 22.

11.   L'atelier qu'il occupa sur la rue Richmond, à London, de 1960 à 1963, n'avait que deux fenêtres. Curnoe estampilla avec un alphabet de tampons de caoutchouc, sur un morceau de toile à tracer (48,2 x 35,5 cm [19 x 14 po]), au cours du printemps 1961, une description du paysage urbain vu de la fenêtre gauche sur le mur ouest. Il s'agit de *Cityscape* qui se trouve dans la collection de M. et Mme David P. Silcox d'Ottawa. L'atelier qu'il occupa ensuite sur la rue King, de 1963 à 1968, comptait sept fenêtres d'où il décrivit systématiquement dans ses tableaux ce qu'il voyait.

CATALOGUE

1

Vue de l'hôpital Victoria, deuxième série (10 février 1969 – 10 mars 1971)

Huile, encre à marquer, graphite, papier de tapisserie collé sur contre-plaqué, métal, plexiglas, haut-parleurs, bande sonore magnétique et texte imprimé dans un cahier de 8 pages (texte original reproduit aux pages 58 à 65).
243,8 x 487,0 cm (96 x 191-3/4 po)
EXPOSITION: Toronto, The Isaacs Gallery, 17 mars – 5 avril 1971, *Greg Curnoe Views of Victoria Hospital and Wings over the Atlantic.*
GALERIE NATIONALE DU CANADA, OTTAWA (16894)
Acheté en 1971

Il existe quatre autres œuvres sur le même thème que la présente. La première est une description du paysage, écrite avec un alphabet de tampons de caoutchouc sur six toiles consécutives de 229,7 x 238,7 cm (118 x 94 po) chacune[12], la deuxième et la troisième, deux enregistrements au magnétophone[13], et la dernière, un collage[14].

A plusieurs reprises depuis 1969, Curnoe a également enregistré dans un ordinateur une autre description du paysage vu, cette fois, depuis la fenêtre située immédiatement à droite du centre du mur nord de son atelier, la même que celle du n° 8 de cette exposition. L'artiste communiquait à partir de son atelier avec l'ordinateur du

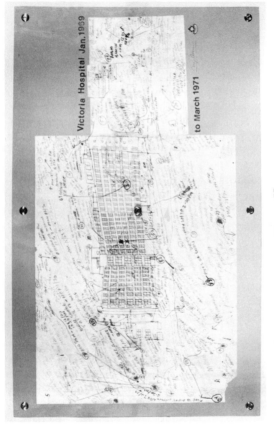

Figure II

département des sciences d'informatique de l'University of Western Ontario de London[15] au moyen d'un téléscripteur relié par téléphone (fig. III).

Pendant les deux années qu'il a peint ce tableau, Curnoe a noté, en ordre chronologique sur une feuille de papier où il avait fait un dessin schématique de l'hôpital dans le paysage (fig. II), ce qu'il a pu observer assis, au hasard des heures passées à regarder par la fenêtre.

La présente œuvre est faite de l'adjonction de trois éléments, de nature différente, décrivant la même scène à trois niveaux de perception: un tableau, un texte et une bande sonore. Le tableau sert de point de convergence aux deux autres éléments. Les numéros éparpillés sur la surface trouvent leur sens dans le texte qui correspond exactement aux notes accumulées sur l'esquisse et qui a été dactylographié par Curnoe dans le cahier qui accompagne le tableau. La bande sonore est entendue à partir de deux haut-parleurs placés aux extrémités supérieures du tableau. Le spectateur, pendant la perception de l'œuvre dans son ensemble, est amené constamment à passer d'un niveau à un autre pour reconstituer, à travers l'appréhension spontanée des éléments visuels, textuels et sonores, non seulement le paysage dans ses détails, mais aussi le désordre même des événements qui se sont produits pendant la fabrication de l'œuvre.

À la vision du tableau, comme à la lecture du texte, se produisent fréquemment, et tout naturellement, une suite de passages d'un sens à un autre et même souvent à l'intérieur d'un seul détail. La bande sonore, même si elle est littérale, n'échappe pas non plus à cette règle de l'ambiguïté des significations.

Ces trois éléments se présentant simultanément, chacun d'eux n'a pleinement son sens que relié aux deux autres. L'analyse d'un élément visuel, par exemple, nous amène forcément à considérer l'élément littéraire qui peut parfois l'expliciter, et l'inverse est aussi vrai.

Le tableau est dominé par l'édifice qui a donné son nom au titre. Le texte, lui, ne nous apprend rien de plus sur sa fonction d'hôpital. Si Curnoe l'a peint si grand, c'est qu'il domine vraiment le paysage réel[16]. Il est entouré d'arbres, de maisons, de champs et d'autres édifices. À sa gauche se trouve une bouteille, à sa droite un avion. Une bande de couleur, surtout rose et mauve, sépare la composition en deux parties à peu près égales et représente le meneau de la fenêtre[17]. Les numéros de la surface représentent l'ordre chronologique du texte qui représente à son tour, des événements qui se sont réellement produits mais qui ne sont pas représentés, en général, par une forme peinte sur le tableau[18].

Chaque tache de couleur représente aussi quelque chose qui était vraiment dans le paysage, sur la vitre de la fenêtre ou même, comme la bouteille, dans l'atelier. Chacun de ces éléments visuels a une importance primordiale pour Greg Curnoe, puisque selon lui on ne peut vraiment connaître l'ensemble d'une chose qu'en l'examinant d'abord dans toutes ses parties. Ainsi, tout ce qui se trouve à l'arrière-plan est ici aussi clairement représenté qu'au premier plan alors que dans la réalité cela devrait être flou. Cette «manie» des détails, l'amène par exemple, à peindre une à une les deux cent dix-huit fenêtres visibles sur la façade de l'hôpital! C'est chez lui, une passion que l'on retrouve aussi chez certains peintres naïfs.

Le choix des couleurs est arbitraire et leur fonction n'est pas toujours réaliste. Ainsi, l'hôpital qui est en réalité construit de briques jaunes, passe ici, entre autres, du jaune au rose, puis au vert pâle et à l'orangé. Quant aux arbres ils sont verts ou jaunes, roses ou bleus. Comme pour confirmer cette attitude vis-à-vis la couleur, le numéro 55 du texte nous avertit quand même que l'arbre ici peint en rose, est en réalité soudainement devenu jaune-orange clair! Ce système se justifie chez Curnoe par l'intuition qu'il a de la fonction même de la couleur qui est de «colorer», sans nécessairement devoir correspondre à la réalité ordinaire. Il lui suffit qu'elle serve à distinguer les formes les unes des autres et surtout qu'elle corresponde à son goût[19].

Tout le tableau, dans sa texture même, fonctionne comme la fenêtre qui lui a servi de point de départ. C'est un objet devant lequel on se place, et au travers duquel on voit simultanément une image et la surface sur laquelle cette image est vue. Alors que les numéros 5, 36, 37, 67 et 97 du texte sous-entendent la transparence de la vitre, la solidité de sa surface et son pouvoir réfléchissant la nuit, le numéro 58 confirme clairement cette métaphore de la surface du tableau en tant que fenêtre; la goutte d'eau dont il est question dans le texte est représentée par la trace d'une goutte de peinture délibérément peinte de haut en bas comme si la surface du tableau[20] avait en quelque sorte la transparence de la fenêtre. Que ce dernier soit aussi tout simplement une surface solide et opaque cela est également signalé clairement dans le texte aux numéros 3 et 80 et de façon beaucoup plus directe[21].

Les notations du texte de Curnoe sont directes et prosaïques, et elles dépendent entièrement de son humeur du moment. Elles sont aussi peu systématiques que le tableau lui-même. C'est un récit fait de fragments, et les événements en ont dicté son déroulement. C'est leur coïncidence avec l'attention visuelle de Curnoe qui est le point de départ du texte.

Les regroupements thématiques que nous pouvons faire à la lecture peuvent trouver une explication qui est souvent aussi prosaïque que les événements eux-mêmes. Par exemple, si Curnoe note aux numéros 12, 14, 16, 20, 39, 40, 41, 42, 43, 44, 51, 54, 65, 68, 69, 72, 73, 78, 90, 97, tant de lumières, c'est qu'il est en fait bien difficile de voir autre chose à travers une fenêtre la nuit. De même, s'il parle plus d'une fois de nuages (25, 48, 57), de fumées (6, 11, 15, 25, 32, 47, 66, 77, 88, 93, 98, 106, 111, 116), d'oiseaux (22, 33, 52, 95, 96, 107, 113) ou d'insectes (19, 34, 35, 50) c'est qu'il est, de fait, impossible de voir autre chose quand on observe ce qui se passe dans l'atmosphère!

Le texte étant aussi un journal personnel, Curnoe, aux numéros 3, 7, 28, 37, 38, 51, 53, 63, 64, 78, 81, 92, 94, 104 et 105, ne ressent pas le besoin de décrire la place exacte de ces personnes dans sa vie chaque fois qu'il en parle. C'est pour cette raison qu'il ne mentionne que des prénoms et des initiales sauf pour une exception[22]. Maintenant que ce texte est publié, il n'est peut-être pas sans intérêt de savoir à qui ils correspondent, suivant l'ordre de leur apparition dans le texte. Owen (Curnoe) est le fils aîné de l'artiste; Jack (Chambers) est un peintre[23]; Jimmy (McRae) est un voisin; Glen (Curnoe) est son frère cadet, bibliothécaire[24]; Archie (Leitch) est un comptable et à l'époque, musicien dans le Nihilist Spasm Band; C(lare) B(ice) est aussi un peintre[25]; Sheila (Curnoe) est l'épouse de Greg, et Galen[26], son fils cadet; Selwyn (Dewdney) est un expert sur la pictographie des indiens du Canada[27] et Irène son épouse, thérapeute par l'art et politicienne; Mary (Rose) est céramiste; Doreen (Curry) est bibliothécaire spécialisée en musique; Hal (Sheftel) était un employé d'une compagnie torontoise de location de projecteurs; enfin Sam, lui, est un chat de la famille Curnoe et qui a disparu depuis.

Dire qui sont ces personnes en décrivant surtout leur activité, explique de façon plausible leur présence dans la vie de l'artiste. Une biographie plus détaillée, même si elle ne correspondait pas aux intentions de Curnoe au moment où il a noté leur nom, servirait à définir plus précisément le milieu culturel dans lequel il évolue.

Le texte est dans son ensemble, une chronique du temps qui passe, et chaque notation est identifiée selon la date et l'heure où elle a été enregistrée. L'accumulation patiente de tous ces détails finit par reconstruire peu à peu la vie du peintre aux moments où il s'est assis devant sa fenêtre et a noté ce qu'il voyait, ce qu'il entendait, ou même, ce qui s'est produit ailleurs que dans l'atelier ou le paysage comme c'est le cas des numéros 104 et 105 et c'est pour cette raison qu'ils ne sont pas peints sur la surface.

Le texte pourrait être commenté numéro par numéro, phrase par phrase, mot par mot, même, et une analyse de ce type recréeraient, comme en archéologie, tout un lieu, toute une époque. Elle nous apprendrait par exemple, quel temps il faisait à telle heure ou à telle date[28], comment les édifices, les rues, l'atelier étaient éclairés, quelle sorte de musique on était susceptible d'entendre[29], comment les gens communiquaient[30], comment ils se véhiculaient, etc.

Ces notes, justement parce qu'elles sont tout à

fait ordinaires, créent par accumulation une somme sur la vie quotidienne. Elles sont, comme la mémoire, un ensemble dont les parties constituantes peuvent, prises séparément, être plus ou moins significatives mais qui trouvent pleinement leur sens dans leur convergence en un centre. Le texte a un premier sens dans sa totalisation, un autre dans sa convergence au tableau et à la bande sonore et finalement, un autre dans ce qu'il révèle de l'individualité de l'auteur qui est son point d'origine.

La bande sonore est le seul élément littéral de la composition. C'est à une date et à une heure précises que les choix de l'emplacement du microphone ont été faits (voir les numéros 26, 27, 28, 29, et 31 du texte). Les bruits que l'on entend sont en général l'effet du pur hasard[31]. C'est de plein gré que l'artiste a choisi ensuite quelle bande sonore allait faire partie de la composition, et deux des cinq bandes enregistrées ont été détruites uniquement à cause de leur mauvaise qualité technique. Par son réalisme absolu, la bande sonore rattache directement l'œuvre au temps et au lieu de sa création. C'est surtout par elle que cette *Vue de l'hôpital Victoria, deuxième série (10 février 1969 – 10 mars 1971)* est à jamais circonstanciée[32].

C'est pendant qu'il peignait le tableau que Greg Curnoe a soudainement eu l'idée d'estampiller la fenêtre d'où il avait tant regardé du mot *Region* dans un cercle. Ce geste a plusieurs significations. C'est pour lui, d'abord et avant tout, une simple plaisanterie. C'est aussi une façon simple de brouiller, en quelque sorte toute distinction entre l'art et la réalité «ordinaire». Curnoe a ensuite répété l'estampille sur le tableau, cette fois soulignée de sa signature elle aussi estampillée, puisqu'elle faisait lors logiquement partie du sujet à peindre. Celle-ci se retrouve sur cinq des sept autres tableaux de cette exposition, puisqu'elle s'est trouvée sur les fenêtres correspondantes à ceux-ci.

Le mot *Region* sur le tableau est aussi une façon de définir l'œuvre. Ce tableau, ce texte, cette bande sonore constituent, fragment par fragment, le portrait d'une région en même temps que celui de l'auteur de l'œuvre.

NOTES

12. *Vue de l'hôpital Victoria, première série: nᵒˢ 1–6 (27 août 1968 – 10 janvier 1969).* Ces tableaux sont à la Galerie nationale du Canada à Ottawa. En faisant la deuxième série, l'artiste, en couvrant du regard le même panorama, s'est efforcé d'inclure à peu près tout ce qu'il avait décrit dans la première.

13. *Vue de l'hôpital Victoria nᵒ 1, troisième série (16 avril 1969, 11 h 45 à 12 h 15 et 17 avril 1969, 8 h 40 à 9 h 10).* Enregistrement stéréophonique sur cassette (collection de l'artiste). Greg Curnoe, dans le catalogue de l'exposition *955,000,* organisée par Lucy R. Lippard à la Vancouver Art Gallery du 13 janvier au 8 février 1970, donne quelques renseignements sur cet enregistrement: «Le microphone fut placé sur une boîte en bois sur le bord de l'ancienne rive de la rivière à 41° 8′ au nord du coin nord-ouest de notre maison . . .» (traduit de l'anglais.)

Il existe un autre enregistrement (collection de l'artiste), du même titre, fait au printemps 1969 et présentée dans une exposition du groupe *The London Survey* à la 20/20 Gallery de London, du 22 avril au 11 mai 1969.

14. *Vue de l'hôpital Victoria, quatrième série (1970–1971),* collection de l'artiste. C'est un collage sur un morceau de plexiglas, découpé selon le profil de l'hôpital.

15. L'ordinateur a même été programmé de façon a pouvoir retransmettre les écrits de Curnoe exactement au même rythme avec les mêmes erreurs de frappe et les mêmes hésitations que celui-ci y a initialement enregistré. C'est avec l'appui enthousiaste de John Hart, directeur du département des sciences d'informatique de l'University of Western Ontario de London que Bill Fraser et Mike Dawdy ont rédigé le programme de l'ordinateur.

Curnoe a présenté deux feuilles de son journal, telles que retransmises par l'ordinateur par téléphone interurbain à un téléscripteur dans l'exposition *45° 30' N − 73° 36' W* à l'université Sir George Williams et The Saidye Bronfman Centre de Montréal, du 1ᵉʳ au 17 février 1971. Le texte de Curnoe dans le catalogue explique brièvement le projet.

16. C'est encore le hasard qui est, en quelque sorte, responsable de la présence de cet hôpital dans son œuvre. Il est visible de toutes fenêtres du mur nord de son atelier, mais ce n'est pas à cause de lui qu'il l'a acheté! Curnoe a déjà pensé, par ironie, à une analogie entre l'hôpital Victoria dans son œuvre et la montagne Sainte-Victoire chez Cézanne!

17. Curnoe a d'ailleurs bien failli oublier de peindre le meneau. Ce n'est qu'à la dernière minute qu'il se rendit compte qu'il avait occupé son champ visuel pendant près de deux ans! Il n'est d'ailleurs pas indiqué sur l'esquisse de la collection Anne Brodsky, Toronto (fig. II).

18. Il y a toutefois une exception au réalisme

du texte. Le numéro 24 explique la présence de l'avion militaire américain en feu dans le ciel de London. Curnoe a, de propos délibéré, présenté cet événement fictif comme réel pour amener le spectateur justement à s'interroger sur sa réalité et donc d'en envisager la probabilité.

19.   Curnoe n'a jamais vraiment démenti cette rumeur, sûrement malveillante, qui a couru dans sa famille et dans les milieux artistiques de London, voulant qu'il soit daltonien. C'est là, sa façon d'affirmer son libre arbitre quant aux couleurs et son refus d'accorder toute valeur objective à celles-ci (c'est-à-dire correspondre à la couleur «réelle» des choses).

20.   Cette trace passe du rose pâle au jaune puis au blanc crémeux. Les autres traces qui se trouvent ici et là sur la surface sont accidentelles.

21.   Cette oscillation perpétuelle entre «la réalité» et le tableau, ce va-et-vient visuel et littéraire entre la tautologie et la métaphore sont démontrées intuitivement par l'emploi du mot *ici* dans le texte.

Alors qu'aux numéros 3 et 80 *ici* désigne uniquement ce qui se trouve *sur* la surface du tableau (cette dernière est *ici* au moment où nous la regardons), aux numéros 7, 38 et 92 il se réfère à ce qui se produit en réalités *là-bas,* dans l'hôpital et aux numéros 95 et 96 à *là-bas* dans le paysage réel.

Le sens d'*ici* au numéro 21 est plus ambigu encore puisqu'il désigne l'atelier et le terrain sur lequel il est situé plutôt que la parcelle de paysage au-dessus de laquelle le numéro est placé.

Au numéro 37 *ici* désigne simultanément la fenêtre et le paysage.

22.   Au numéro 67 apparaît le nom d'un célèbre ancien joueur de hockey du club Canadien de Montréal, *Jean Béliveau.* Il sert de marque de

commerce à un jouet pour enfants qui se trouve dans l'atelier de l'artiste.

23. À partir de photographies, prises du toit de l'atelier de Curnoe, Chambers a peint, en 1969–1970, une vue réaliste de l'hôpital Victoria dans un paysage d'hiver. C'est un tableau dont l'atmosphère silencieuse et mélancolique est l'antihèse de celui peint par Curnoe.

24. W. Glen Curnoe est aussi l'auteur de *Around London 1900–1950, A Picture History,* imprimé à compte d'auteur, London, 1973.

25. Clare Bice est aussi l'ancien conservateur de la London Public Library and Art Gallery (Ontario).

26. Les deux incidents des numéros 104 et 105 furent surtout malheureux pour le fils cadet de l'artiste Galen, alors âgé de trois ans, parce qu'ils se produisirent à deux jours d'intervalle.

27. Selwyn Dewney est le co-auteur avec Kenneth E. Kidd de *Indian Rock Paintings of the Great Lakes,* University of Toronto, Press, Toronto, 1967.

28. Les quatre saisons de chacune des deux années sont même représentées simultanément sur le tableau.

29. Au numéro 118, *Syrinx* est le nom d'un groupe de trois musiciens, John Mills Cockell, Doug Pringle et Allan Wells. Le disque qu'ils ont enregistré, en 1970, pour True North de Toronto s'intitule aussi *Syrinx* et c'est de celui-ci qu'il s'agit ici. Le groupe Syrinx a aussi, en 1971, enregistré un disque pour la même compagnie, *Long Lost Relative.*

30. Voir les numéros 18, 37, 38, 53, 63, 64, 78, 79, 81 et 92.

31. Il y a certaines exceptions comme les coups de bâtons sur un couvercle de métal devant

le microphone gauche puis devant celui de droite et les coups de pistolet jouet qui suivent de près des bruits d'avions inattendus.

32.   Le premier côté de la cassette stéréophonique d'une durée de cent vingt minutes correspond au numéro 28 du texte avec une légère variante en ce qui concerne l'heure de l'enregistrement. Quant au deuxième côté de la cassette il est celui du numéro 29 du texte. Sur la cassette, Curnoe a inscrit: «Micro sur la clôture directement sous deux cheminées – tel que vu de la fenêtre du N.-0., 20 h 15 à 21 h 15, 9 août 1970, 22 h 25 à 23 h 25, 16 août 1970.» (traduction de l'anglais).

Curnoe a l'intention de remplacer cet enregistrement en reliant le tableau, accroché à la Galerie nationale du Canada à Ottawa, directement par téléphone, à un microphone qui serait placé au même endroit derrière l'atelier.

2

Vue de la fenêtre la plus au nord sur le mur est
(15 mars 1969 – 17 septembre 1969)

Acrylique, encre à marquer, papier de tapisserie
collé sur contre-plaqué, haut-parleur, et bande
sonore magnétique
226,0 x 256,5 cm (89 x 101 po), dimensions maxi-
mums, incluant le haut-parleur
EXPOSITION: Toronto, The Isaacs Gallery, 17 mars
– 5 avril, 1971, *Greg Curnoe Views of Victoria
Hospital and Wings over the Atlantic.*
ONTARIO HERITAGE FOUNDATION, TORONTO

Les différents mots estampillés sur le tableau in-
diquent où et quand les objets peints ont été
achetés à London. C'est Hugh McIntyre, un membre du Nihilist Spasm Band, qui a fabriqué le
«Hugh's Kazoo», un instrument de musique qui
resta dans l'atelier de l'artiste quand le groupe
déménagea en 1965 pour se produire plus ou
moins régulièrement les lundis soir dans les tavernes de la ville.

   La forme en éventail du tableau résulte de l'uti-
lisation des restes du contre-plaqué employé en
1967–1968 par Curnoe pour la fabrication d'un
objet de forme pyramidale, intitulé *Kamikaze.*

   Le haut-parleur diffuse des bruits enregistrés
sous la fenêtre, dehors, le 19 juin 1969 de 13 h 30
à 14 h 30 et de 21 h à 22 h. Le papier de tapisserie
que Curnoe utilise dans tous les tableaux de cette
exposition est un papier pré-collé, commercial et
domestique choisi pour sa qualité ordinaire.

3

Vue de la fenêtre la plus à l'est sur le mur nord
(5 mai 1969 – 18 décembre 1969)

Acrylique, encre à marquer, papier de tapisserie
collé sur contre-plaqué, haut-parleur et bande
sonore magnétique
274,3 x 122,0 cm (108 x 48 po) haut-parleur
inclus
EXPOSITION: Toronto, The Isaacs Gallery, 17 mars
– 5 avril 1971, *Greg Curnoe Views of Victoria
Hospital and Wings over the Atlantic.*
L'ARTISTE PAR L'ENTREMISE DE THE ISAACS GAL-
LERY, TORONTO

Dans cette œuvre le haut-parleur occupe une
position identique à celle que le microphone avait
dans l'atelier, suspendu du plafond, lors des enregistrements de la bande magnétique, le ven-
dredi 16 mai 1969, de 11 h 15 à 12 h 15 et le
samedi 17 mai 1969, de 13 h 55 à 14 h 55.
Un autre ruban magnétique enregistré le 30
juillet 1970 à 13 h 41 et à 14 h 30 pour ce tableau
ne fut pas utilisé.
 L'objet identifié par le mot «EVERLAST» est
un casque de boxeur. En bas et au centre du tableau la forme représentée est un cornet d'un
ancien gramophone utilisé par l'artiste pour fa-
briquer l'un de ses «kazoo».
 Greg Curnoe admire particulièrement la sim-
plicité et la franchise des écrits du savant suisse
Auguste Piccard et la citation estampillée en bas
et à droite du tableau est une traduction tirée
d'un de ses livres, *Entre terre et ciel* (édition

Ouchy, Lausanne, 1946). Le texte original (p. 129–130) est: «Au-dessus de l'horizon, le ciel. D'abord, la troposphère vue dans toute son étendue, laiteuse, presque blanche tout près de l'horizon. Un peu plus haut, le ciel comme nous le connaissons. Encore plus haut, la limite entre troposphère et stratosphère, la tropopause, est bien visible. Plus haut, c'est la stratosphère. Elle tranche nettement de la troposphère par sa limpidité parfaite. Elle est bleue, d'un bleu foncé, de plus en plus foncé si nous élevons le regard. Plus haut, elle devient violacée. Nous avons déjà tous vu cette couleur pourprée de la stratosphère, le matin très tôt ou le soir quand, pour un observateur terrestre, le soleil est encore au-dessous de l'horizon. Seule la stratosphère est éclairée et elle n'est pas bleu ciel, mais d'un mélange de bleu et de rouge.»

4

*Vue de la fenêtre la plus au sud sur le mur est
(10 novembre 1969 – janvier 1970)*

Acrylique, encre à marquer, papier de tapisserie
collé sur contre-plaqué, haut-parleur et bande
sonore magnétique
71,1 x 208,3 cm (28 x 82 po)
EXPOSITION: Toronto, The Isaacs Gallery, 17
mars – 5 avril 1971, *Greg Curnoe Views of
Victoria Hospital and Wings over the Atlantic.*
M. E. J. ESCAF, LAMBETH, ONTARIO

Le bois utilisé dans la fabrication de ce tableau
provient d'une caisse d'emballage. C'est par es-
tampillage que tous les textes ont été écrits. Ils
nous renseignent sur les objects qui sont placés
dans l'atelier, à gauche de la fenêtre. De haut en
bas on peut lire (trad.): «*Sony F99S / microphone*»; ensuite: «Photographie supérieure en
noir et blanc de *Len's Brough* sur une carte
postale»; suivi de: «Endos d'une formule de la
B(anque) de *M*(ontréal) avec une note sur la
foire des bricoleurs et *Walt Disney* écrite au
crayon»; puis de: «Lettre de *R*(ichard) *Hamilton*
avec instructions pour *Highgate* manuscrite par
moi»; et enfin: «*Morandi,* calendrier *Olivetti,
1967*».

À gauche du tableau l'estampille *more trivia/
no allegory again!!* ([trad.]: encore des banalités,
toujours pas d'allégorie!!) est un commentaire
ironique de Curnoe sur la vue de la fenêtre et sa
propre peinture. Il y exprime son dégoût marqué

de l'allégorie et des tentatives de trouver un sens
«profond» à son art.

Précédant des flèches le mot *ASA* est le nom
d'une chatte de la famille Curnoe qui fut tuée par
une automobile pendant la fabrication du
tableau.

Curnoe parle de la chatte dans la première
partie de la bande sonore de soixante minutes,
enregistrée le 2 décembre 1969 à 23 h 50. La
deuxième partie est un enregistrement d'une
partie de hockey, diffusée, de Toronto, le 3 décembre 1969 à 21 h 55 ou 22 h 55 sur un récepteur de
radio placé en haut et à droite de la fenêtre.

5

Vue de la fenêtre à gauche du centre sur le mur nord (23 juin – 21 août 1970)

Acrylique, encre à marquer, papier de tapisserie collé sur contre-plaqué, haut-parleur et bande sonore magnétique
187,0 x 171,5 cm (73-5/8 x 67-1/2 po) haut-parleur inclus
EXPOSITION: Toronto, The Isaacs Gallery, 17 mars – 5 avril 1971, *Greg Curnoe Views of Victoria Hospital and Wings over the Atlantic.*
THE ALUMNI ASSOCIATION OF THE UNIVERSITY OF WESTERN ONTARIO, LONDON, ONTARIO

Le morceau de papier représenté au centre du tableau est un menu du restaurant Mackie's situé sur la plage de Port Stanley sur la rive du lac Érié, près de London. Ce restaurant est peinturé d'un motif orange et bleu que Curnoe aime beaucoup.

Le texte estampillé explique comment le carreau de la fenêtre a été cassé (trad.): «Comment la fenêtre fut brisée! J'avais appuyé la dernière section de la clôture en piquets bleus contre la cheminée parce que le jeune voisin avait marché dessus dans le gazon! Elle fut ou bien poussée par le vent ou renversée et elle frappa la vitre en tombant! Écrit le *20* août *1970* à 15 h 10!»

Pour enregistrer la bande sonore le microphone a été placé dehors sur un escabeau à droite de la fenêtre le 20 août 1970 de 22 h à 23 h et le 23 août 1970 de 5 h 40 à 6 h 40. Curnoe a aussi cassé une vitre pendant l'enregistrement.

6

Vue de la fenêtre la plus au nord sur le mur ouest (22 octobre 1970 – 10 mars 1971)

Acrylique, encre à marquer, papier de tapisserie collé sur contre-plaqué, haut-parleurs et bande sonore magnétique
122,0 x 304,8 cm (48 x 120 po)
EXPOSITION: Toronto, The Isaacs Gallery, 17 mars – 5 avril 1971, *Greg Curnoe Views of Victoria and Wings over the Atlantic.*
Dʳ M. ROBINSON, LONDON, ONTARIO

Les bouteilles peintes sur le bas du tableau font toutes partie de la collection de l'artiste. Le texte estampillé indique le lieu d'origine et la date d'acquisition de chacune d'entre elles.

L'objet représenté au centre du tableau est une photographie aérienne de l'hôpital Victoria de London (Ontario), publiée dans *The London Free Press,* avec un système de numérotage semblable à celui que Curnoe utilisa dans *Vue de l'hôpital Victoria, deuxième série (10 février 1969 – 10 mars 1971).* Il ignorait l'existence de cette photographie que Murray Favro, un artiste de London, lui donna après qu'il eût terminé son grand paysage (cat. nᵒ 1).

Sur la partie supérieure gauche du tableau, la main de l'artiste tient une photographie de Michel Chartrand, président du Conseil central de Montréal qui est affilié à la Confédération des syndicats nationaux (CSN), ainsi que deux citations estampillées: *It's their one world American horse shit/C'est leur universelle merde améri-*

caine, et *Know thr th steam roller on your face/ Apprends par le rouleau à vapeur sur ton visage.* Elles ont été tirées d'un poème de Bill Bissett, de Vancouver, intitulé *Love of Life th 49th Parallel.* Il a été écrit en 1970 et publié originalement par la Blewointment Press de Vancouver, puis a paru, en 1971, dans un recueil de poème du même auteur, *Nobody owns th earth,* chez Anansi à Toronto.

Pour l'enregistrement de cette bande sonore réalisée le samedi 6 mars 1971, de 10 h 40 à 11 h 25 et le lundi 8 mars 1971, de 12 h à 12 h 45, le microphone était dans l'atelier sur une table de ping-pong à 10 pieds (3,05 m) de la fenêtre.

7

Vue de la fenêtre au-dessus des portes doubles dans le mur est, 1971

Acrylique, encre à marquer et papier de tapisserie collé sur contre-plaqué
61,6 x 122,6 cm (24-1/4 x 48-1/4 po)
EXPOSITION: Toronto, The Isaacs Gallery, 25 janvier – 13 février 1973, *Greg Curnoe* (sous le titre, *Vue de la fenêtre au-dessus des portes doubles dans le mur ouest* [et non *est*]).
LA BANQUE D'ART, CONSEIL DES ARTS DU CANADA, OTTAWA

Le texte estampillé à droite est de Curnoe (trad.): «Gris ou gris?? Zénith. La brise s'est levée. Le ciel est couvert – gris pâle avec de faibles lignes de gris plus pâle encore. Il fait à peu près *70* degrés dehors. Toutes les feuilles bougent dans les arbres, je peux les entendre même si la porte sous cette fenêtre est fermée. Le vent s'amplifie. Il y a une forte impression de soulagement dans le ciel. Les nuages gris plus foncé se dirigent vers l'est très rapidement sous le couvert d'un gris plus pâle. 11 h 55 – 15 septembre – *1971*.»
L'orthographe du mot «GREY» ([trad.]: gris) est délibérément anglaise plutôt qu'américaine.

8

Vue de la fenêtre à droite du centre sur le mur nord (24 août 1971 – 21 janvier 1973)

Huile, encre à marquer, papier de tapisserie collé sur contre-plaqué, haut-parleur et bande sonore magnétique
182,9 x 122,0 cm (72 x 48 po) tige et haut-parleur 48,3 cm (19 po)
EXPOSITION: Toronto, The Isaacs Gallery, 25 janvier – 13 février 1973, *Greg Curnoe.*
CITY SAVINGS AND TRUST COMPANY, VANCOUVER, COLOMBIE-BRITANNIQUE

Les circonstances de l'enregistrement de la bande sonore sont décrites dans le texte estampillé sur la partie inférieure gauche de la fenêtre. (trad.): «Mon dactylo est sur la table sous la fenêtre décrite sur ce tableau. Mardi *16* janvier de 11 h 30 à midi et *18* janvier de 9 h 30 à 10 h. J'ai dactylographié une description de la vue de la fenêtre, avec le magnétophone en marche et le microphone accroché à un clou sur le châssis de la fenêtre, juste au-dessus du dactylo.»

Dans la partie supérieure droite du tableau une guêpe, vue de profil, ainsi qu'une autre identique mais en bas à droite, ont été imprimées à l'aide d'une étampe de caoutchouc appartenant à Owen, le fils aîné de l'artiste. Pour les autres insectes, Curnoe utilisa une étampe de caoutchouc différente, tirée d'un dessin qu'il fit spécialement pour ce tableau.

Le thermomètre publicitaire de la compagnie Almatex, fabricant de l'émail jaune clair préféré de Curnoe, est représenté à gauche de la fenêtre. C'est un cadeau de ses amis Don et Bernice Vincent lors de son installation dans l'atelier actuel.

La forme bleue au centre sur la partie inférieure du tableau est un fragment de lampe en verre bleu-outremer placé sur la vitre de la fenêtre. Ce morceau à la même intensité de bleu translucide que la bouteille de Bromo peinte dans la *Vue de l'hôpital Victoria, deuxième série (10 février 1969 – 10 mars 1971)*, voir catalogue n° 1. C'est une couleur que l'artiste aime aussi beaucoup.

C'est aussi de cette fenêtre que Curnoe enregistre son journal sur ordinateur.

EXPOSITIONS

(*Expositions individuelles de Greg Curnoe et expositions de groupe choisies; ces dernières se distinguent par un astérisque.*)

*Toronto, The Garret Gallery, décembre 1957 (groupe de neuf artistes).

London (Ontario), Richard E. Crouch Branch Library, 3–30 novembre 1961, *Exhibitions of Things*.

*London (Ontario), Region Gallery, 1962 (?), *Greg Curnoe, Larry Russell*.

*London (Ontario), Region Gallery, mars 1963, *Greg Curnoe, Brian Dibb*.

*London (Ontario), The McIntosh Memorial Art Gallery, University of Western Ontario, 26 novembre – 19 décembre 1962, *Mr. Curnoe and Mrs. Cumming*.

Toronto, Gallery Moos, 12–30 septembre 1963, *Greg Curnoe*.

Toronto, David Mirvish Gallery, 17 septembre – 6 octobre 1964, *Greg Curnoe, «STUFF»*.

*Regina, Norman Mackenzie Art Gallery, 8–31 octobre 1964, *John Chambers, Greg Curnoe* (avec catalogue).

*London (Ontario), The McIntosh Memorial Art Gallery, University of Western Ontario, 9–27 novembre 1964, *Imports and Local Art Work Curnoe Urquhart*.

Vancouver, Art Gallery, 8–27 février 1966, et Edmonton, Art Gallery, 5–31 mars 1966, *Paintings by Greg Curnoe* (avec catalogues).

Toronto, The Isaacs Gallery, 16 novembre – 5 décembre 1966, *New Work From Sowesto Greg Curnoe*.

Vancouver, The New Design Gallery, 16 novembre – 5 décembre 1966, *Recent Collages by Greg Curnoe*.

London (Ontario), 20/20 Gallery, 15 février – 5 mars 1967, *G. Curnoe's Series*.

Toronto, The Isaacs Gallery, 4–18 avril 1967, *G. Curnoe's time series*.

*London (Ontario), The McIntosh Memorial Art Gal-

lery, University of Western Ontario, 30 octobre –
11 novembre 1967, *Chambers and Curnoe Art
Exhibit* (*avec catalogue*).

*Regina, Norman Mackenzie Art Gallery, 16 novembre
– 17 décembre 1967, *Statements: 18 Canadian
Artists* (avec catalogue).

*Paris, Musée national d'art moderne, 12 janvier –
18 février 1968, *Canada. Art d'aujourd'hui.* L'exposition fut ensuite présentée à Rome, Lausanne et
Bruxelles (avec catalogue).

*Édimbourg, College of Art, International Festival,
18 août – 7 septembre 1968, *Canada 101* (avec catalogue).

*Ottawa, Galerie nationale du Canada, 1968–1969,
Cœur de London. Exposition itinérante (avec catalogue).

Toronto, The Isaacs Gallery, 5–24 février 1969, *Greg
Curnoe.*

*London (Ontario), 20/20 Gallery, 22 avril – 11 mai
1969, *The London Survey.* Exposition de groupe:
Margo Arris, Don Bellamy, Don Bonham, Jack
Chambers, Tom Coulter, Greg Curnoe, Kee Dewdney,
Paterson Ewen, Murray Favro, R. Fenwick.

*Vancouver, Art Gallery, 13 janvier – 8 février 1970,
955,000 (avec catalogue).

London (Ontario), The McIntosh Memorial Art Gallery,
University of Western Ontario, 2–19 avril 1970, *Greg
Curnoe Drawings.*

Toronto, The Isaacs Gallery, 29 avril – 18 mai 1970,
Greg Curnoe . . . Collages 1961–70.

*Montréal, Sir George Williams University et The
Saidye Bronfman Centre, 1er–17 février 1971, *45° 30'
N – 73° 36' W* (avec catalogue).

Toronto, The Isaacs Gallery, 17 mars – 5 avril 1971,
*Greg Curnoe Views of Victoria Hospital and
Wings over the Atlantic.*

Montréal, Waddington Galleries, 16 novembre –
4 décembre 1971, *Greg Curnoe.*

London (Ontario), The London House, 1er–7 février
1972, *Greg Curnoe – Display of Water Colours
Measurements and Clockings.*

Toronto, The Isaacs Gallery, 25 janvier – 13 février 1973, *Greg Curnoe.*

London (Ontario), The Polyglot Gallery, 14 juin – 5 juillet 1973, *Greg Curnoe – Watercolours and drawings.*

Ottawa, Galerie nationale du Canada, 1974–1975, *The Great Canadian Sonnet, Dessins de Greg Curnoe* (exposition itinerante avec catalogue).

London (Ontario), The Forest City Art Gallery, 16 novembre – 4 décembre 1974, *Greg Curnoe Watercolours.*

Toronto, The Isaacs Gallery, 4–21 février 1975, *Greg Curnoe Recent Watercolours.*

London (Ontario), London Art Gallery, 5–28 septembre 1975, *Greg Curnoe Some Lettered Works, 1961–1969.*

ÉCRITS DE GREG CURNOE, EN ORDRE CHRONOLOGIQUE

Sans titre, daté 15 janvier 1961, dans *Region,* n° 1 (1961), n.p.

Sans titre, daté 26 mars 1961, dans *Region,* n° 1 (1961), n.p.

Statement, dans *Region,* n° 2 (janvier 1962), p. 5.

About Wearing My Dead Grandfather's Glasses, dans *Region,* n° 3 (1962), n.p.

Hangover, dans *Region,* n° 3 (1962), n.p.

Steering Wheel, dans *Region,* n° 4 (septembre 1962), n.p.

Confessions of an ex Bicycle Rider, dans *Region,* n° 5 (février 1963), p. 2.

Region = Regionalism, lettre à la rédaction, dans *The University of Western Ontario Gazette* de London (Ontario), 15 mars 1963, p. 9.

Sans titre, dans *Region,* n° 6 (1963?) n.p.

Préface, catalogue d'exposition, *Walt Redinger: Sculptor, Ed Zelenak: Sculptor, John Boyle: Painter,*

London (Ontario), The McIntosh Memorial Art Gallery, 22 février – 12 mars 1964.

Selections from 3rd Trip to Montreal, dans *Region,* n° 7 (juin 1964), p. 32–34.

Mirrors and Images from the Coke Book, dans *Alphabet,* n° 9 (novembre 1964), p. 43–47.

Greg Curnoe 1936–, texte dans un article en collaboration, *Ten artists in search of Canadian art,* dans *Canadian Art,* t. XXIII, n° 1, livraison n° 100 (janvier 1966), p. 64.

Not Leftover Art, lettre à la rédaction, dans *The London Free Press* de London (Ontario), 12 juillet 1966.

Sans titre, éditorial, dans *Region,* n° 8 (été 1966), n.p.

Radio Journal. Rubrique dans *20 Cents Magazine,* t. I, n° 2 (octobre 1966), n.p.

A Conversation About Mixed Media From New York City as Seen at The University of Western Ontario Nov. 17 and McMaster University, Nov. 12, 1966, dans *20 Cents Magazine,* t. I, n° 3 (octobre – novembre 1966), n.p.

Sans titre, lettre à la rédaction, dans *20 Cents Magazine,* t. I, n° 4 (décembre 1966), n.p.

Radio Journal. Rubrique dans *20 Cents Magazine,* t. I, n° 4 (décembre 1966), n.p.

Radio Journal. Rubrique dans *20 Cents Magazine,* t. I, n° 5 (janvier 1967), n.p.

Sans titre, lettre à la rédaction, dans *20 Cents Magazine,* t. I, n° 5 (janvier 1967), n.p. (Réimpression d'une lettre à la rédaction dans *The University of Western Ontario Gazette* de London (Ontario), 15 mars 1963.)

Boyling Point, dans *20 Cents Magazine,* t. I, n° 6 (février 1967), n.p.

Radio Journal. Rubrique dans *20 Cents Magazine,* t. I, n° 6 (février 1967), n.p.

Radio Journal. Rubrique dans *20 Cents Magazine,* t. I, n° 7 (mars 1967), n.p.

Notes – on the North Wall, dans *Region,* n° 9 (printemps 1967), n.p.

Radio Journal. Rubrique dans *20 Cents Magazine,* t. I, n° 8 (avril 1967), n.p.

Radio Journal. Rubrique dans *20 Cents Magazine,* t. I, n° 9 (mai 1967), n.p.

Sans titre, texte dans le catalogue de l'exposition, *Statements: 18 Canadian Artists,* Regina, Norman Mackenzie Art Gallery, 16 novembre – 17 décembre 1967, p. 38–42.

Radio Journal. Rubrique dans *20 Cents Magazine,* t. II, n° 3 (décembre (?) 1967), n.p.

Radio Journal. Rubrique dans *20 Cents Magazine,* t. II, n° 4 (mars (?) 1968), n.p.

Radio Journal. Rubrique dans *20 Cents Magazine,* t. II, n° 5 (juin (?) 1968), p. 7.

Radio Journal. Rubrique dans *20 Cents Magazine,* t. II, n° 6 (juillet (?) 1968), p. 33–35.

Radio Journal. Rubrique dans *20 Cents Magazine,* t. III, nos 3–4 (mai 1969), n.p.

N.E. Thing Co. Conference. Article sous la rubrique *Radio Journal,* dans *20 Cents Magazine,* t. III, nos 5–6 (juin 1969), n.p.

N.E. Thing Co. Conference (Part Two). Article sous la rubrique *Radio Journal,* dans *20 Cents Magazine,* t. III, nos 7–8 (octobre 1969), p. 20.

Greg Curnoe (from journals written on the C.N.R. on the way to Toronto, 8:55 or so, Wednesday morning, August 13, 1969). Cité (p. 25) dans l'article de Mendes Ross: *The Language of the Eyes Windows and Mirrors,* dans *Artscanada,* t. XXVI, n° 5, livraison n° 136/137 (octobre 1969), p. 20–25.

N.E. Thing Co. Conference (Part Three). Article sous la rubrique *Radio Journal,* dans *20 Cents Magazine,* t. III, n° 9 (novembre 1969), p. 20.

The Coke Book Continued, dans *Alphabet,* n° 17 (décembre 1969), p. 20.

Excerpts from Wings Over the Atlantic. Article sous la rubrique *Radio Journal,* dans *20 Cents Magazine,* t. III, n° 10 (décembre 1969), p. 20.

Questions posées par Greg Curnoe et citations, dans *Greg Curnoe Canada.* Catalogue par Dennis Reid pour la Xe biennale, São Paulo (Brésil), 1969, p. 68.

Sans titre, texte et citations, dans *955,000.* Catalogue par Lucy Lippard (édit.) pour Art Gallery, Vancouver, 13 janvier – 8 février 1970.

Radio Journal. Rubrique dans *20 Cents Magazine,* t. IV, n° 1 (janvier 1970), p. 20.

The Mothers of Invention – Ron Bowman and Greg Curnoe in Conversation. Article sous la rubrique *Radio Journal,* dans *20 Cents Maga-zine,* t. IV, n° 2 (février 1970), n.p.

Greg Curnoe's Radio Journal. Rubrique dans *20 Cents Magazine,* t. IV, n° 3 (mars 1970), n.p.

Amendments to Continental Refusal/Refus Con-tinental, dans *20 Cents Magazine,* t. IV, n° 4 (avril 1970), n.p.

Greg Curnoe's Radio Journal. Rubrique dans *20 Cents Magazine,* t. IV, n° 4 (avril 1970), n.p.

Greg Curnoe's Radio Journal. Rubrique dans *20 Cents Magazine,* t. IV, n°s 5–6 (juin 1970), n.p.

Préface, catalogue de l'exposition, *Inventions and Perpetual Motion Machines,* London (Ontario), 20/20 Gallery, 2–21 juin 1970.

Greg Curnoe's Radio Journal. Rubrique dans *20 Cents Magazine,* t. IV, n° 7 (septembre 1970), p. 20.

Curnoe on London, dans *The London Free Press* de London (Ontario), 17 octobre 1970.

The most beautiful book in the world (critique de *the Economic Atlas of Ontario, Toronto, 1970*), dans *Artscanada,* t. XXVII, n° 6, livraison n° 150/151 (décembre 1970 – janvier 1971), p. 64-65.

(Avec McFadden [David]): *The Great Canadian Son-net,* Coach House, Toronto, 1970. Illustrations par Greg Curnoe.

En collaboration, *Snore Comix, Bright Things,* Coach House, Toronto, 1970.

Sans titre, textes de Greg Curnoe p. 7 et 76, dans *The cosmic chef an evening of concrete,* Nichol, B. P. (édit), Ottawa: Oberon, 1970.

Sans titre, texte dans *45° 30′ N – 73° 36′ W.* Catalogue de l'exposition par Gary Coward, Bill Vazan, Arthur Bardo et Zoe Notkin (édit.), Montréal, université Sir

George Williams et The Saidye Bronfman Centre, 1er–17 février 1971.

Kasabonika – Simmons – Thomas – Curry – Dic – St. Germain – Patterson – Stansell – Laithwaite, etc. Rapport dactylographié sur l'art populaire pour le Musée national de l'homme, Ottawa, octobre 1970 – mars 1971.

En collaboration, *Open Letter to W. O. Twaits, Chairman, Imperial Oil Ltd.* Communiqué polycopié pour une manifestation, Ottawa, 27 mai 1971.

Notes on Picabia, dans *Artscanada,* t. XXVIII, n° 4, livraison n° 158/159 (août–septembre 1971), p. 70–71.

(Avec Bozak [Bob]): *Artists dispute Fanshawe College statement,* lettre à la rédaction dans *The London Free Press* de London (Ontario), 2 novembre 1971.

Art Purchase, lettre à la rédaction, *The London Free Press* de London (Ontario), 4 janvier 1972.

Critique de *The Projector* de M. Vaughn-James (Toronto: 1971), dans *The Canadian Forum,* t. LII, n° 617 (juin 1972), p. 40, 41.

(Avec Théberge [Pierre]): *For Dan Patterson and Arthème St. Germain/Pour Dan Patterson et Arthème St-Germain.* Manifeste de l'Association pour la documentation des aspects négligés de la culture au Canada. Feuillet polycopié, 8 août 1972. Publié dans *La Revue de l'Association pour la Documentation des Aspects Négligés de la Culture au Canada,* t. 1, n° 1, p. 1.

From the Blue Book/Journals, dans *Open Letter,* Second Series, n° 4 (printemps 1973), p. 94–108.

Notebook Greg Curnoe, dans *Proof Only,* t. 1, n° 1 (15 novembre 1973), p. 2–3.

Canadian Painters, lettre à la rédaction, dans *The Globe and Mail* de Toronto, 26 novembre 1973.

David McFadden, dans *The Great Canadian Sonnet Dessins de Greg Curnoe,* catalogue d'exposition, Ottawa, Galerie nationale du Canada, 1974, n.p.

(Avec Bergeron [Léandre]): *A Bi-Focus on Barry Lord: The History of Painting in Canada,* dans

Books in Canada, t. 3, n° 8 (décembre 1974), p. 20,
36–38.

The Dilemma of Provincialism A History of Canadian Painting (critique de Dennis Reid: A Concise
History of Canadian Painting, Toronto, 1973),
dans The Canadian Forum, t. 54, n° 648 (février
1975), p. 30–32.

Sans titre, dans Greg Curnoe Some Lettered Works,
1961–1969, catalogue d'exposition, London (Ontario),
London Art Gallery, 5–28 septembre 1975, p. 1–4.

BIBLIOGRAPHIE CHOISIE

An artistic affront to Americans, éditorial, dans The
London Free Press de London (Ontario), 2 avril
1968, p. 6.

Bisset (Bill): Nobody owns th   earth, Anansi, Toronto, 1971.

Bodolai (Joe): Borderlines in Art and Experience,
dans Artscanada, t. XXXI, n° 1, livraison
n° 188/189 (printemps 1974), p. 65-81.

Boyle (John B.): Continental Refusal/Refus Continental, dans 20 Cents Magazine, t. IV, n° 4
(avril 1970), n.p.

Chandler (John Noel): More Words on Curnoe's
Wordly World, dans Artscanada, t. XXVI, n° 2,
livraison n° 130/131 (avril 1969), p. 3–8.

———. Painting «From Life»: Greg Curnoe at the
Isaacs Gallery Ltd, dans Artscanada, t. XXVIII,
n° 3, livraison n° 156/157 (juin-juillet 1971), p. 75.

———. sources are resources: Greg Curnoe's objects, objectives and objections, dans Artscanada, t. XXX, n° 1, livraison n° 176/177 (février–mars
1973), p. 69.

Cobb (David): A Man of Involvement, dans Toronto
Daily Star de Toronto, 14 septembre 1963, p. 29.

Coleman (Victor): Knowing: the surface, dans Artscanada, t. XXIX, n° 1, livraison n° 164/165 (février –
mars 1972), p. 71, 72.

Crawford (Lenore): *Spoofs Reveal Artist, Odd Objects Exhibit Startles Art Lovers*, dans *The London Free Press* de London (Ontario), 4 novembre 1961.

————. *G. Curnoe and K. T. Cumming at the McIntosh Memorial Art Gallery, University of Western Ontario*, London, dans *Canadian Art*, t. XX, n° 2, livraison n° 84 (mars–avril 1963), p.86,87

————. *Londoners step up invasion of Montreal Art Galleries*, dans *The London Free Press* de London (Ontario), 4 avril 1964.

————. *Urquhart, Curnoe exhibit a mixture of color, vitality, humor*, dans *The London Free Press* de London (Ontario), 14 novembre 1964, p. 21.

————. *Artist Curnoe more «Involved» than ever*, dans *The London Free Press* de London (Ontario), 3 décembre 1966.

————. *«The Spasms»*, dans *The London Free Press* de London (Ontario), 3 février 1968, p. 35.

————. *«Before storm»*, dans *The London Free Press* de London (Ontario), 30 mars 1968.

————. *Curnoe art dominates new show*, dans *The London Free Press* de London (Ontario), 21 juillet 1970.

————. *Curnoe displays art in Toronto*, dans *The London Free Press* de London (Ontario), 20 mars 1971.

————. *Canada buys Curnoe work*, dans *The London Free Press* de London (Ontario), 14 août 1971.

————. *Curnoe «on the spot» water-colors show «first» for old hotel*, dans *The London Free Press* de London (Ontario), 2 février 1972.

————. *Curnoe reveals superb new talent*, dans *The London Free Press* de London (Ontario), 25 juin 1973.

Curnoe – A File Interview, dans *File*, t. II, n°s 1–2 (avril–mai 1973), p. 46, 47 et 61.

Curnoe At The Front, dans *Georgia Straight*, de Vancouver, 6–13 juin 1974.

Dault (Gary, Michael): *Heart of London*, dans *Arts-*

canada, t. XXV, n° 4, livraison n° 122/123 (octobre–novembre 1968), p. 43.

――――. *Greg Curnoe's love of bicycles expressed in beautiful paintings,* dans *The Toronto Star,* de Toronto, 7 février 1975.

Davis (Rae): *The Life of death in London,* dans *Canadian Art,* t. XXIII, n° 3, livraison n° 102 (juillet 1966), p. 20–25, 50–51.

Hale (Barry): *Stick around and work with what's around you,* dans *Saturday Night,* t. LXXXV, n° 1, livraison n° 3499 (janvier 1970), p. 25–29.

Harris (Marjorie): *Nihilist Spasm Band,* dans *Arts-canada,* t. XXV, n° 2, livraison n° 118/119 (juin 1968), p. 6, 7.

Kidd (Bruce): *Bruce Kidd interviews Greg Curnoe,* dans *The Canadian Forum,* t. LIII, n° 631 (août 1973), p. 22–30.

Lord (Barry): *Painters Became Politically Aware in '68,* dans *Kitchener-Waterloo Record* de Kitchener-Waterloo (Ontario), 28 décembre 1968.

――――. *What London, Ontario has that everywhere else needs,* dans *Art in America,* t. LVII, n° 5 (septembre-octobre 1969), p. 103–105.

――――. *The History of Painting in Canada, Toward a People's Art,* N. C. Press, Toronto 1974.

McFadden (David): *The Great Canadian Sonnet,* illustré par Greg Curnoe, Coach House, Toronto, 1970.

――――. *Au sujet de Greg Curnoe, artiste,* dans *The Great Canadian Sonnet Dessins de Greg Curnoe,* catalogue d'exposition, Ottawa, Galerie nationale du Canada, 1974.

McKenzie (Robert C.): *Beaver kosmos: A Narrow-minded Review,* dans *20 Cents Magazine,* t. I, n° 8 (avril 1967), n.p.

――――. *Greg Curnoe's Connexions,* dans *20 Cents Magazine,* t. IV, n° 3 (mars 1970), n.p.

McPherson (Hugo): *Greg Curnoe's Shorthand,* dans *20 Cents Magazine,* t. I, n° 6 (février 1967), n.p.

Mendes (Ross): *The language of the eyes–Windows and Mirrors,* dans *Artscanada,* t. XXVI, n° 5, livraison n° 136/137 (octobre 1969), p. 20–25.

Oille (Jennifer): *Greg Curnoe at the Isaacs Gallery*, dans *Only Paper Today*, t. 2, n° 6, mars 1975, p. 2.

Parker (Harley): *Greg Curnoe's paintings: Moos Gallery, Toronto (September 12 – October 2)*, dans *Alphabet*, n° 7 (décembre 1963), p. 87–89.

Pratten (Art): *Note from the «Art Editor»*, dans *20 Cents Magazine*, t. I, n° 8 (avril 1967), n.p.

Pringle (Douglas): *The Great Canadian Sonnet*, dans *Artscanada*, t. XXVII, n° 4, livraison n° 146/147 (août 1970), p. 71, 72.

Rabinowitch (Royden): *Nihilists Co-operate*, dans *20 Cents Magazine*, t. I, n° 4 (décembre 1966), n.p.

Rans (Geoffrey): *A Word (Sotto Voce) About The Region: inside my picket fence in London, Ontario*, dans *20 Cents Magazine*, t. I, n° 5 (janvier 1967), n.p.

———. *20/20 Gallery: A Report and a Prediction*, dans *20 Cents Magazine*, t. I, n° 8 (avril 1967), n.p.

Reaney (James): *Introduction* au catalogue d'exposition, *John Chambers, Greg Curnoe*, Regina, Norman Mackenzie Art Gallery, 8–31 octobre 1964.

———. *Role of the inscription in painting*, dans *Canadian Art*, t. XXIII, n° 4, livraison n° 103 (octobre 1966), p. 41–45.

Reid (Dennis): *Greg Curnoe Canada*, catalogue d'exposition pour la Xe biennale, São Paulo (Brésil), Galerie nationale du Canada, Ottawa, 1969.

———. *A Concise History of Canadian Painting*, Oxford University Press, Toronto, 1973.

Robillard (Yves): *L'affaire de la murale de l'aéroport de Dorval*, dans *La Presse* de Montréal, 6 avril 1968.

Rockman (Arnold): *Greg Curnoe at the Gallery Moos, Toronto*, dans *Canadian Art*, t. XXI, n° 1, livraison n° 89 (janvier–fevrier 1964), p. 10.

«69»: *The object Was to Paint (Print?) 24 Panels, One An Hour For 24 Hours, From 12:00 a.m. Wednesday, December 14th, to 12:00 a.m. Thursday, December 15th. The Panels Were 10 by 10 Sheets of Tin Plate With Lapped Edges*, dans *20 Cents Magazine*, t. I, n° 4 (décembre 1966), n.p.

Théberge (Pierre): *Confessions of a Nihilist Spasm Band Addict,* dans *Artscanada,* t. XXVI, n° 6, livraison n° 138/139 (décembre 1969), p. 67, 68.

―――. *Soixante dessins de Greg Curnoe pour The Great Canadian Sonnet de David McFadden, «. . . beau(x) . . . comme la rencontre fortuite sur une table de dissection d'une machine à coudre et d'un parapluie!»* (*Lautréamont*), dans *The Great Canadian Sonnet Dessins de Greg Curnoe,* catalogue d'exposition, Ottawa, Galerie nationale du Canada, 1974.

Thompson (David): *A Canadian scene: 3,* dans *Studio International,* t. CLXXVI, n° 906 (décembre 1968), p. 241–245.

Wallace (Helen): *Remove objectionable Curnoe airport art,* dans *The London Free Press* de London (Ontario), 28 mars 1968, p. 31.

―――. *Anti-American work by Curnoe removed from Dorval Airport mural,* dans *The London Free Press* de London (Ontario), 29 mars 1968, p. 1, 10.

―――. *While controversy rages,* dans The London *Free Press* de London (Ontario), 30 mars 1968.

The Weekly Interview, Greg Curnoe (*Part I*), dans *The London Weekly* de London (Ontario), 16 juillet 1968.

The Weekly Interview, Greg Curnoe (*Part II*), dans *The London Weekly* de London (Ontario), 23 juillet 1968.

Woodman (Ross): *Greg Curnoe.* Introduction sur feuillet polycopié pour l'exposition *Greg Curnoe Series,* London (Ontario), 20/20 Gallery, 15 février–5 mars 1967.

―――. *London* (*Ont.*): *a new regionalism,* dans *Artscanada,* t. XXIV, n° 8–9, livraison n° 111/112 (août–septembre 1967), encart n.p.

―――. *London: regional liberation front,* dans *The Globe and Mail* de Toronto, 13 décembre 1969.

CANADA

GREG CURNOE

XXXVII International Biennial Exhibition
of Art, Venice, 1976

Organized by the National Gallery of Canada,
Ottawa
A National Museum of Canada

LENDERS

The Alumni Association of the University of Western Ontario, London, Ontario

The Art Bank, Canada Council, Ottawa, Ontario

The Artist, through The Isaacs Gallery, Toronto, Ontario

City Savings and Trust Company, Vancouver, British Columbia

Mr E. J. Escaf, Lambeth, Ontario

Ontario Heritage Foundation, Toronto

Dr M. Robinson, London, Ontario

PREFACE

This is the twelfth time Canada has exhibited at the Venice *Biennale*. On this occasion a commissioner from the Province of Quebec, Pierre Théberge, Curatorial Administrator at the National Gallery of Canada, has chosen the work of a painter from the Province of Ontario, Greg Curnoe, and has written about him with enthusiasm in the catalogue. In organizing this exhibition we are very much indebted to the lenders from as far away as British Columbia on the west coast of Canada for making it possible for the National Gallery to show the liveliest and strongest examples of Curnoe's works in Venice. As always, in exhibiting abroad, the National Gallery is very much indebted to the Cultural Affairs Division of Canada's Department of External Affairs for its collaboration, and in particular here for the help of its Embassy in Rome. It is also very grateful for the assistance of the Italian Embassy in Ottawa.

Jean Sutherland Boggs
Director
The National Gallery of Canada, Ottawa

Figure I

INTRODUCTION

Greg Curnoe lives in London, Ontario, where he was born in 1936. London is a city with a population of 225,000 located in the south-west of the province, and it has a very lively artistic milieu.

Curnoe is a writer as well as a painter; for years, he has been concurrently keeping several journals in which he regularly writes his observations on every-day life.[1] He has also founded and edited the magazine *Region* – published in London from 1961 to 1967 – and from 1966 to 1970 regularly collaborated with the *20 Cents Magazine,* which was also published in London.

Greg Curnoe has also made films.[2]

A keen collector, he has accumulated, among other things, soft-drink bottles manufactured by small firms from all corners of Canada,[3] geographic maps of the country, bicycles, cycling magazines, books on dirigibles and "Big Little Books,"[4] topographical instruments, and a large number of contemporary folk-music records.

Greg Curnoe is also an amateur bicycle racer.[5]

He is passionately interested in popular culture in all its manifestations and is an active member of the Association for the Documentation of Neglected Aspects of Culture in Canada of which he was the co-founder in 1972, and for which he has amassed a large collection of slides on popular art.[6]

He is also a member of a food co-operative, and of the Forest City Art Gallery of London – an artists' co-operative founded in December 1973. As well, he was one of the founders of three other co-operatives, the first in Toronto – The Garrett

Gallery (1957–1959), and two others in London –the Region Gallery (1961–1963), and the 20/20 Gallery (1966–1970).

Curnoe is at present the Ontario provincial spokesman for CAR (Canadian Artists Representation), a national association of Canadian artists. He was a founding member and is one of the presidents of the Nihilist Party of London,[7] which devotes all its energy to the organization of a picnic and an annual banquet for its members. On 1 July 1975 he was made artist-in-residence for a year at the University of Western Ontario in London.

As a musician, Curnoe plays the kazoo with the Nihilist Spasm Band,[8] a noise-making band which since 1965 has played regularly on Monday nights in the beer-halls of London, and which is currently playing in London at the Forest City Art Gallery.

Curnoe is a confirmed regionalist and a militant spokesman for anti-Americanism; it is in this capacity that he wrote the manifesto *Refus continental,* published in 1969,[9] with the painter John Boyle from St Catharines, Ontario.

Greg Curnoe is married and has three children.

All of Greg Curnoe's work is autobiographical. He has deliberately chosen to limit his field of activity to his region – London, Ontario – and his themes are generally drawn from this source. For Greg Curnoe, the only possible culture is regional, and the only genuine form of art springs from daily experience. His painting is spontaneous, without a system, and presents whatever holds his passing attention for one reason or another. Greg Curnoe considers himself an artisan, a *bricoleur,* a completely subjective observer of reality. Only one principle motivates him: the pleasure he finds in doing what he does. Greg Curnoe wants his art to be an integral part of his life, and to reflect as much as possible all that interests him.[10]

Since 1968, he has occupied a studio which has eight windows placed on three of its four walls (fig. I). The paintings which appear here correspond to these eight windows, and continue the long series of works, begun in 1961, describing what he saw from the windows of his two previous studios. As well, these works all reflect a common outlook: the benevolent study of reality, framed as it were by accidents of construction.[11]

NOTES

1.   The *Coach House Press* publishing house in Toronto is preparing a facsimile edition in five volumes of one of these journals, *The Blue Book,* written from August 1964 to March 1967. Curnoe is still working on this series. The publishing of another one, *The Coke Book,* is in the preparation stage with Alphabet Press in London, Ontario. Curnoe is also concurrently keeping an "audio journal" on cassettes. He made his first recording on 19 March 1968 during an automobile trip from London, Ontario, to Montreal, with the poet Robert Fones.

2.   He has made two films: the first one, *Sowesto* (1947–1969), is a 16 mm silent film, in colour, lasting 30 minutes; the second, *Connexions* (1969–1970), is a 16 mm film with sound-track, in colour, lasting 15 minutes.

3.   One of the reasons that these bottles are important to Curnoe is that they demonstrate the existence of regional cultures in Canada. The shapes of the bottles and the design of the brand names vary from one region to another, and even

their taste, within the same recipe – "cream soda" or "spruce beer" for example – is different according to the brand and place of origin, which indicates precise regional preferences.

4. Illustrated children's books, published mostly during the forties.

The Great Canadian Sonnet by David McFadden was published in 1970 in the "Big Little Books" format and following its principle. Curnoe illustrated this book with one hundred and ninety-four drawings. The concept characteristic of this series – illustrations outlined in black accompanied with a caption – was to allow children to "read" the book independently of the text.

5. In the fall of 1973 he won a trophy from a cycling club, the London Centennial Wheelers, not because he was a good cyclist, but because he had regularly participated in the weekly races they organized. On the other hand, he designed and had made in 1975 the jerseys for the club members.

In 1972, before finishing his paintings of views from the eight windows of his current studio on Weston Street, Curnoe made a series of "portraits" of two of his bicycles – the 1951 "C.C.M." and the "Zeus" – using acrylic on plywood cut in the shape of the bicycle. In 1973, he undertook another series of "portraits" of all his bicycles, still life-size, but this time using water-colours on rectangular paper; in the same year, he also began a third series of "portraits" of bicycle wheels on square paper.

6. According to its manifesto, the goal of this association is to "blur the artificial border between the 'fine' arts and culture;" some day, it intends to publish the photographic documents it is accumulating. Pierre Théberge is its co-founder

and co-president. Between 6 December 1974 and 2 January 1975, the association presented more than six hundred slides of "neglected" objects to the Public Library and Art Museum of London, Ontario, and published the first issue of its review on this occasion.

7.   The word "NO" is the only programme of the Nihilist Party. All its members are its simultaneous presidents.

8.   The kazoo is a type of wind instrument. The Nihilist Spasm Band in 1968 cut a record with the Allied Record Corporation of Toronto. This band also played in Paris during the VIᵉ Biennale des jeunes, and at the Institute of Contemporary Art in London, England, in October 1969. In addition to Curnoe, it was then composed of six other musicians: John B. Boyle, William A. Exley, Murray Favro, Archie Leitch, Hugh McIntyre, and Art Pratten. Except for the drums, the instruments are the inventions of members of the band.

9.   The title of the manifesto paraphrases the *Refus global* by Paul-Émile Borduas, published in 1948.

Furthermore, this attitude caused him certain difficulties when it was expressed in his work: for example, a mural commissioned by the Department of Transport of the Canadian government in 1968 for Montreal's international airport at Dorval was never installed because of its anti-Americanism (the mural is currently on extended loan to the National Gallery of Canada in Ottawa); and a project commissioned by a tobacco company for a mural to be painted on a building in Toronto was rejected for the same reason.

Curnoe refuses to exhibit his work in the United States.

10. B.K. "Do you intend to preserve every moment of your life?"

G.C. "Well, I'm not preserving every moment, I couldn't do that. That would mean that all my waking hours would be spent preserving. I'm just doing things that I find interesting." (From an interview by Bruce Kidd, "Bruce Kidd interviews Greg Curnoe," in *The Canadian Forum*, vol. LIII, no. 631 [August 1973], p. 22.)

11. The studio which he occupied on Richmond Street in London from 1960 to 1963 had only two windows; during the spring of 1961, using a piece of tracing cloth (19 x 14 in. [48.2 x 35.5 cm]) and a rubber-stamp alphabet, Curnoe made a description of the urban landscape viewed from the left window on the west wall. (*Cityscape*, collection of Mr and Mrs David P. Silcox of Ottawa.) His next studio on King Street, where he worked from 1963 to 1968, had seven windows; he systematically described in his paintings what he saw from each of them.

CATALOGUE

1

View of Victoria Hospital, Second Series (February 10, 1969–March 10, 1971)

Oil, marking ink, pencil, and wall-paper on plywood, metal, plexiglas, loudspeakers, magnetic sound tape, eight-page printed text (reproduced on pp. 58–65)
243.8 x 487.0 cm (96 x 191-3/4 in.)
EXHIBITION: Toronto, The Isaacs Gallery, 17 March–5 April 1971, *Greg Curnoe Views of Victoria Hospital and Wings over the Atlantic.*
THE NATIONAL GALLERY OF CANADA, OTTAWA (16894)
(Purchased in 1971)

There are four other works on the same theme as this one: the first is a description of the view, written with a rubber-stamp alphabet on six[12] consecutive canvases, each measuring 299.7 x 238.7 cm (118 x 94 in.); the second and the third are recordings;[13] the fourth is a collage.[14]

Several times since 1969 Curnoe has also recorded on a computer another description of the scene, this time from the window located immediately to the right of the centre of the north wall of his studio (no. 8 in this exhibition). The artist communicated from his studio with a computer at the Department of Computer Sciences at the

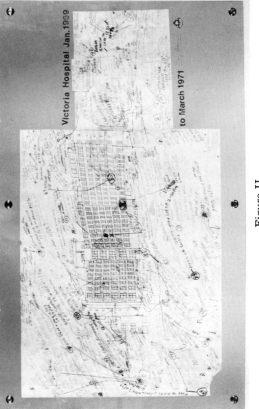

Victoria Hospital Jan.1959 to March 1971

Figure II

134

University of Western Ontario in London[15] by using a terminal connected by telephone (fig. III).

During the two years which he took to make this painting, Curnoe noted in chronological order on a sheet of paper – on which he had drawn a sketch of the hospital and surrounding landscape (fig. II) – what he was able to observe while sitting looking out the window.

This work is the combination of three quite different elements which describe the same scene at three levels of perception: a painting, a text, and a sound-track. The picture becomes the point at which the two other elements converge. The numbers scattered over the painting are explained in the text which Curnoe has typed in a note-book, which accompanies the painting and which corresponds exactly to the notes accumulated on the sketch. The sound-track is heard from two loudspeakers placed at the top extremities of the picture. While perceiving the work as a whole, the spectator is constantly led to switch from one level to another to recreate, through the spontaneous perception of the visual, textual, and acoustic elements, not only the scene in its details, but also the disorder of the events which occurred during the production of the work by Curnoe.

When viewing the picture and while reading the text, a series of different meanings frequently happens quite naturally, and often within a single detail. Even if it is literal, the sound-track does not escape from this rule of ambiguity.

Because these three elements appear simultaneously, the full meaning of each of them can only be appreciated in relation to the two others. For example, the analysis of the visual element inevitably leads us to consider the literary element which could explain it, and the reverse is also true.

The picture is dominated by the building named in the title. The text tells us nothing more of its function as a hospital; Curnoe painted it so big because it really dominates the actual scene.[16] It is surrounded by trees, fields, houses, and other buildings. In the picture, there is a bottle to its left, and an airplane to its right. A coloured strip, mostly pink and purple, separates the composition into two almost equal parts and represents the mullion of the window.[17] The numbers represent the chronological order of the text, which in turn represents events which actually occurred – but which are usually not represented by a shape on the surface.

Each spot of colour represents something which was actually in the scene, on the window-pane, or even, like the bottle, in the studio. Each of these visual elements is of primordial import-ance to Greg Curnoe, since, in his opinion, some-thing can only be understood by examining it first in all its parts; thus, everything in the back-ground – which should be slightly blurred in reality – is here represented as clearly as are objects in the foreground. This "mania" for detail leads him, for example, to paint the two hundred and eighteen windows visible on the back façade of the hospital one by one! His approach is simi-lar to the passion for detail in certain naïve painters.

The choice of colours is arbitrary, and their function is not always realistic: the colour of the hospital, for example, which in reality is con-structed of yellow bricks, can vary here from yellow to pink, to light green and then to orange; the trees are green or yellow, pink or blue. To confirm this attitude towards colour, number 55 of the text advises us that the tree – painted here in pink – has in reality suddenly become a bright yellow-orange! Curnoe justifies this system by his intuition of the function of colour, which is to "colour," without necessarily having to correspond to reality for him. It is sufficient that it separates forms from one another, and moreover, corresponds to his taste.[19]

The entire painting, even in its texture, works in the same way as its starting point, the window: it is an object in front of which we stand, and through which we simultaneously see an image and the surface on which this image is painted. Whereas numbers 5, 36, 37, 67, and 97 of the text suggest the transparency of the window-pane, the solidity of its surface, and its power to reflect at night, number 58 clearly confirms this metaphor of the surface of the painting as a window. The drop of water, mentioned in the text, is represented by the trace of a drop of paint painted deliberately from top to bottom on the surface of the painting,[20] as if the painting had the transparency of the window. That the painting is also quite simply a solid and opaque surface is just as clearly noted in the text – in a much more direct manner – at numbers 3 and 80.[21]

The notations in Curnoe's text are direct and prosaic, and depend entirely on his mood of the moment. They are as unsystematic as the painting itself. It is a story composed of fragments, and events have dictated its plot; their coincidence with Curnoe's visual attention is the origin of the text.

The thematic groups – which can be made when reading the text – offer an explanation which is often as prosaic as the events themselves. For example, if Curnoe records so many lights at numbers 12, 14, 16, 20, 39, 40, 41, 42, 43,

44, 51, 54, 65, 68, 69, 72, 73, 78, 90, and 97, it is because it is hard to see anything else through a window at night; if he talks more than once about clouds (numbers 25, 48, and 57), smoke (numbers 6, 11, 15, 25, 32, 47, 66, 77, 88, 93, 98, 106, 111, and 116), birds (numbers 22, 33, 52, 95, 96, 107, and 113), or insects (numbers 19, 34, 35, and 50), it is because, in fact, it is impossible to see anything else when observing what goes on in the air.

At numbers 3, 7, 28, 37, 38, 51, 53, 63, 64, 78, 81, 92, 94, 104, and 105, Curnoe only mentions first names and initials (with one exception)[22] without explaining to whom they belong; the reason is that this text is also a personal journal, and he does not feel the need to describe the exact place of these people in his life each time he mentions them. Now that this text is published, it is perhaps interesting to know to whom these names belong, listed in the order of their appearance in the text: Owen (Curnoe) is the artist's eldest son; Jack (Chambers) is a painter;[23] Jimmy (McRae) is a neighbour; Glen (Curnoe) is his younger brother, a librarian;[24] Archie (Leitch) is an accountant and, at the time, a musician in the Nihilist Spasm Band; C(lare) B(ice) is also a painter;[25] Sheila (Curnoe) is Greg's wife, and Galen[26] is his young son; Selwyn (Dewdney) is an expert on the pictography of Canadian Indians[27] and Irene is his wife, an art-therapist and a politician; Mary (Rose) is a potter; Doreen (Curry) is a librarian specialized in music; Hal (Sheftel) was an employee of a Toronto company which leases searchlights; finally, Sam is a cat which belonged to the Curnoe family and which has since disappeared!

To indicate, even briefly, who these people are – mostly by describing what they do – explains somewhat the significance of their presence in Greg Curnoe's life. A more detailed biography of each of them, even if it did not correspond to Curnoe's intentions when he noted their names, would serve to define more precisely his cultural milieu.

In all, the text is a chronicle of passing time, and each notation is identified by the date and the hour when it was recorded. The patient accumulation of all these details serves to reconstruct little by little the painter's life when he sat down before his window and noted what he saw, heard – or even what happened elsewhere than in the studio or in the landscape, as is the case in numbers 104 and 105 (this is why they are not painted on the surface).

The text could be commented upon entry by entry, sentence by sentence, even word by word, and an analysis of this type would recreate, as in archæology, an entire location, an entire epoch. It would tell us, for example, about the weather at a certain hour or on a certain date,[28] how the buildings, streets, or the studio were lit, what kind of music could be heard,[29] how people communicated,[30] how they moved around, etc.

Precisely because they are quite ordinary, these notes create by accumulation a sum of data on daily life. Like the memory, this text is a whole, of which the components can, when taken individually, be more or less significant; but the full significance of the text is revealed when all the components converge at a centre. One meaning is to be found in the sum total of its parts; another in its relation to the picture and to the sound-track; and is a third meaning found in what it reveals about the individuality of the author.

The sound-track is the only literal element of the composition. The positioning of the microphone was made at a precise date and time (as explained in numbers 26, 27, 28, 29, and 31 of the text), and the noises heard usually occurred by chance.[31] Curnoe then chose which sound-track would be part of the composition, and two of the five tape recordings were destroyed solely because of their bad technical quality. By its absolute realism, the sound-track binds, *View of Victoria Hospital, Second Series (February 10, 1969–March 10, 1971)* directly, and, above all forever, to the time and place of its creation.[32]

It was while painting this work that Greg Curnoe suddenly decided to stamp the word "Region" in a circle on the window through which he had been looking so often. This gesture has several meanings: first and above all, it is simply irony on the part of the artist; it is also a simple way to blur any distinction between art and "normal" reality. This stamping is found again on the painting, this time underlined by his signature (also stamped, as in five of the seven other paintings of this exhibition, since it is to be found on the corresponding windows), because it was then a logical part of the subject to be painted.

The word "Region" on the painting is also a way of defining the work: this painting, this text, this sound-track, constitute, detail by detail, the portrait of a region as well as of the author of the work.

12. *View of Victoria Hospital, First Series: nos 1–6 (August 27, 1968–January 10, 1969).* These paintings are at the National Gallery of Canada, Ottawa. In the second series, by observing the same scene the artist tried to include almost everything he had described in the first.

13. *View of Victoria Hospital no. 1, Third Series (April 16, 1969, 11:45 am–12:15 pm and April 17, 1969, 8:40 am to 9:10 am).* Stereophonic recording on tape (collection of the artist).

In the catalogue of the exhibition *955,000* organized by Lucy R. Lippard, shown at the Vancouver Art Gallery (13 January to 8 February 1970), Curnoe gives some information about the recording: "The microphone was placed on a wooden box on the edge of the old river bank 41° 8' north of the N.W. corner of our place...."

There is another recording (collection of the artist) with the same title; made in the spring of 1969, it was presented in an exhibition of the group *The London Survey* at the 20/20 Gallery from 22 April to 11 May 1969.

14. *View of Victoria Hospital, Fourth Series (1970–1971).* In the collection of the artist. Collage on a piece of plexiglas cut in the shape of the hospital.

15. The computer was even programmed to re-transmit Curnoe's words at exactly the same rhythm (with the same typing errors, the same hesitations) with which he had originally recorded them. Bill Frazer and Mike Dawdy wrote the computer programme, with the enthusiastic support of John Hart, Director of the Department of Computer Sciences of the University of Western Ontario.

Curnoe transmitted two sheets of his journal from the computer by long-distance telephone to a terminal in the exhibition *45° 30′N–73° 36′W*, held at Sir George Williams University and at The Saidye Bronfman Centre in Montreal, from 1 to 17 February 1971. Curnoe's text in the catalogue briefly explains the project.

16.   Chance is again in a way responsible for the presence of this hospital in his work; it is visible from all the windows on the north wall of his studio, but this is not the reason that he bought it! Curnoe has already thought, by obtuse irony, of an analogy between Victoria Hospital in his work and Montagne Sainte-Victoire in Cézanne's work!

17.   Curnoe almost forgot to paint the mullion; it was only at the last minute that he realized it had been before his eyes for nearly two years! It does not appear on the sketch in the collection of Anne Brodsky, Toronto (fig. II).

18.   Still, there is an exception to the realism of the text: number 24 explains the presence of the American military plane burning in the London sky. Curnoe deliberately presented this fictional event as real to lead the spectator to question its reality, and therefore to envision its probability.

19.   Curnoe never really denied this surely malicious rumour – which circulated in his family and in the artistic circles of London – that he was colour-blind; it is his way of asserting his freedom regarding colours, and his refusal to grant any objective value to them (that is, to correspond to the "real" colour of things).

20.   This trace of paint changes in colour from light pink to yellow, and then to creamy white; the other traces of paint which can be found here and there on the surface are accidental.

21.   This perpetual oscillation between "reality"

and the painting, this visual and literary alternation of tautology and metaphor, are intuitively demonstrated by the use of the word "here" in the text.

Whereas "here" in numbers 3 and 80 indicates solely what is found "on" the surface of the painting (which is "here" at the time of our observation), in numbers 7, 38, and 92, it refers to what is happening "there," in the hospital, and in numbers 95 and 96, what is happening "there" in the actual landscape.

The meaning of "here" in number 21 is even more ambiguous, because it designates the studio, and the land on which it is located, rather than the fragment of the landscape above which the number appears.

In number 37, "here" designates at once the window and the landscape.

22.   The name Jean Béliveau, which appears in number 67, belongs to a famous former hockey player with Montreal Canadiens club; it is the brand name of a child's toy in the artist's studio.

23.   In 1969–1970, Chambers painted a realistic view of Victoria Hospital in a winter scene from colour photographs which he took on the roof of Curnoe's studio. This painting, with its silent and brooding feeling, is the antithesis of Curnoe's paintings.

24.   W. Glen Curnoe is also the author of *Around London 1900–1950 A Picture History* (London: privately printed, 1973).

25.   Clare Bice is also the former curator of the London Public Library and Art Gallery, in London, Ontario.

26.   The two incidents in numbers 104 and 105 were particularly unfortunate for Galen, who was

then three years old, because they occurred within two days of each other.

27.   Selwyn Dewdney is the co-author, with Kenneth E. Kidd, of *Indian Rock Paintings of the Great Lakes* (Toronto: University of Toronto Press, 1967).

28.   The four seasons of each of the two years are even represented on the painting simultaneously.

29.   At number 118, "Syrinx" is the name of a group of three musicians, John Mills Cockell, Doug Pringle, and Allan Wells. The record which they cut with True North in Toronto in 1970 is also entitled "Syrinx," and this is what is being referred to. "Syrinx" also released *Long Lost Relative* with True North in 1971.

30.   See numbers 18, 37, 38, 53, 63, 64, 78, 79, 81, and 92.

31.   There are some exceptions: blows with a stick on a metal lid in front of the left microphone, and then the right one, and toy-gun shots which closely follow unexpected airplane sounds.

32.   The first side of the stereophonic tape lasting one hundred and twenty minutes corresponds, with a slight variation in the recording time, to number 28 of the text, and the second side corresponds to number 29. On the cassette, Curnoe wrote: "Mike on fence directly below 2 chimneys –as seen from N.W. window/10:25 pm to 11:25 pm Aug 16–1970/8:15 pm to 9:15 pm Aug 9–1970."

Curnoe intends to replace this recording by directly connecting by telephone the painting hung at the National Gallery of Canada in Ottawa to a microphone which would be placed at the same spot behind the studio.

2

View from the Most Northerly Window on the East Wall (March 15, 1969–September 17, 1969)

Acrylic, marking ink, and wall-paper on plywood, loudspeaker, magnetic sound tape
Maximum dimensions, including loudspeaker: 226 x 256.5 cm (89 x 101 in.)
EXHIBITION: Toronto, The Isaacs Gallery, 17 March–5 April 1971, *Greg Curnoe Views of Victoria Hospital and Wings over the Atlantic.*
ONTARIO HERITAGE FOUNDATION, TORONTO

The inscriptions stamped on the surface of the painting indicate where and when the objects painted were purchased in London. "Hugh's Kazoo" is a musical instrument built by Hugh McIntyre, a member of the Nihilist Spasm Band; it was left in the artist's studio after the band moved in 1965 to play more or less regularly on Monday evenings in London beer-halls.

The fan shape of the painting is determined by the fact that it was built with pieces of plywood which remained in the studio after Curnoe built the pyramidal object entitled *Kamikaze* in 1967–1968.

The loudspeaker plays sounds recorded outside, under the window, on 19 June 1969, from 1:30 pm to 2:30 pm and from 9:0 pm to 10:00 pm. The wall-paper which Curnoe uses in all the paintings in this exhibition is pre-pasted commercial paper, a domestic product chosen for its ordinary quality.

3

View from the Most Easterly Window on the North Wall (May 5–December 18, 1969)

Acrylic, marking ink, and wall-paper on plywood, loudspeaker, magnetic sound tape
274.3 x 122.0 cm (108 x 48 in.), including loudspeaker
EXHIBITION: Toronto, The Isaacs Gallery, 17 March–5 April 1971, *Greg Curnoe Views of Victoria Hospital and Wings over the Atlantic.*
THE ARTIST, THROUGH THE ISAACS GALLERY, TORONTO

The position of the loudspeaker above the painting corresponds to the position of the microphone hanging from the ceiling of the studio during the recording of the sound-track from 11:15 am to 12:15 pm Friday, 16 May 1969, and from 1:55 pm to 2:55 pm Saturday, 17 May 1969. Another tape recorded for this painting on 30 July 1970 at 1:41 pm and at 2:30 pm was not used.

The object identified by the word "EVER-LAST" is a boxer's helmet; the shape in the centre at the bottom of the painting represents the horn of an old gramaphone which Curnoe used in building one of his kazoos.

The quotation stamped at the bottom right of the painting is from the Swiss scientist Auguste Piccard, whose writing Curnoe particularly admires for its simplicity and candour; it reads:

" 'Above the horizon lies the sky. First the troposphere in its entirety, milky almost white next to the horizon. A little higher up is the sky as we know it. Still higher up, the boundary between troposphere and stratosph

ere, or tropopause, is clearly seen. Farther up is the str
atosphere. Its perfect clearness makes it contrast dis
tinctly with the troposphere. It is blue, a dark blue, beco
ming darker and darker as we look higher up. Still higher
up it becomes violet. We have already all seen this pur
ple colour of the stratosphere, very early in the morning
or in the evening when, for an observer on earth, the sun
is still below the horizon. The stratosphere alone is lit
up & not of a sky blue colour, but of a mixture of blue &
red.' Auguste Piccard . . . .
from BETWEEN EARTH & SKY."

4

View from the Most Southerly Window on the East Wall (November 10, 1969–January 1970)

Acrylic, marking ink, and wall-paper on plywood, loudspeaker, magnetic sound tape
71.1 x 208.3 cm (28 x 82 in.)
EXHIBITION: Toronto, The Isaacs Gallery, 17 March–5 April 1971, *Greg Curnoe Views of Victoria Hospital and Wings over the Atlantic.*
MR E.J. ESCAF, LAMBETH, ONTARIO

The wood used in the production of this painting comes from a packing-case. The text has all been stamped on, and describes the objects in the studio which are actually placed to the left of the window. Reading from the top to the bottom, we see:

"Sony F99S microphone"

"Len's Brough Superior B&W photo on postcard"

"back of B of M check form with a note about the Hobby Fair & Walt Disney, written in pencil."

"letter from R. Hamilton, with handwritten directions to Highgate by me."

"Morandi, Olivetti calendar 1967."

The stamp *more trivia no allegory again!!* is an ironic comment by the artist on the view from the window and on his own work. He is also expressing his pronounced dislike of allegory, and of attempts to find a "profound" meaning in his art.

"ASA" (preceding the arrows) is the name of

a cat which belonged to the Curnoe family, and which was killed by an automobile during the production of the painting.

The sound-track lasts sixty minutes. The first part, in which Curnoe talks about the cat, was recorded at 11:50 pm on 2 December 1969. The second part is a recording of a hockey game, broadcast from Toronto on 3 December 1969 at 9:55 pm or 10:55 pm on a radio placed above the window to the right.

5

View from the Left Centre Window on the North Wall (June 23–August 21, 1970)

Acrylic, marking ink, and wall-paper on plywood, loudspeaker and magnetic sound tape
187.0 x 171.5 cm (73-5/8 x 67-1/2 in.), including loudspeaker
EXHIBITION: Toronto, The Isaacs Galle., 17 March–5 April 1971, *Greg Curnoe Views of Victoria Hospital and Wings over the Atlantic*.
THE UNIVERSITY OF WESTERN ONTARIO ALUMNI ASSOCIATION, LONDON, ONTARIO

The piece of paper shown at the centre of the painting is a menu from Mackie's restaurant, located on the beach at Port Stanley on Lake Erie near London, Ontario. This restaurant is painted in an orange and blue pattern which Curnoe likes very much.

The stamped text explains how the window-pane was broken:

"THE WAY THE WINDOW GOT BROKEN! I HAD LEANED THE REMAINING SECTION OF BLUE PICKET FENCE UP AGAINST THE CHIMNEY BECAUSE THE BOY NEXT DOOR HAD BEEN WALKING ON IT IN THE GRASS! IT WAS EITHER BLOWN OR KNOCKED OVER AND IN FALLING HIT THE GLASS! WRITTEN ON AUG. 20, 1970 AT 3:10 P.M.!"

The sound-track was recorded by putting the microphone outside on a step-ladder to the right of the window on 20 August 1970 from 10:00 pm to 11:00 pm, and on 23 August 1970 from 5:40 am to 6:40 am. Curnoe also broke a piece of glass during the recording.

6

View from the Most Northerly Window on the West Wall (October 22, 1970–March 10, 1971)

Acrylic, marking ink, and wall-paper on plywood, loudspeakers, magnetic sound tape
122.0 x 304.8 cm (48 x 120 in.)
EXHIBITION: Toronto, The Isaacs Gallery, 17 March–5 April 1971, *Greg Curnoe Views of Victoria Hospital and Wings over the Atlantic.*
DR M. ROBINSON, LONDON, ONTARIO

The bottles painted at the bottom of the painting are all from Curnoe's collection, and the stamped text indicates which Canadian cities they came from and in what year they were acquired.

The object shown in the centre of the painting is an aerial photograph of Victoria Hospital in London, Ontario, which was published in *The London Free Press* using a number system similar to the one used by the artist in the *View of Victoria Hospital, Second Series (February 10, 1969 –March 10, 1971)*. Curnoe was unaware of the existence of this photograph; the London artist Murray Favro gave it to him after he had finished the large landscape (cat. no. 1).

The upper left section of the painting shows the artist's hand holding a photograph of Michel Chartrand, president of the Conseil central de Montréal, which is affiliated with the Confédération des syndicats nationaux (CSN). The two stamped quotations – *It's their one world American horse shit/C'est leur universelle merde américaine,* and *Know thr th steam roller on your* face/*Apprends par le rouleau à vapeur sur ton visage* – were taken from a poem by Bill Bissett, of Vancouver, entitled "Love of Life th 49th Parallel." Written in 1970, it was originally published by Blewointment Press of Vancouver, and then published in 1971 by Anansi in Toronto in *Nobody owns th Earth,* a collection of poems by Bissett.

The sound-track was recorded by placing the microphone in the studio on a ping-pong table 10 feet (3.05 m) from the window, from 10:40 am to 11:25 am on Saturday 6 March 1971, and from 12:00 pm to 12:45 pm on Monday 8 March 1971.

7

View from Window above the Double Doors in the East Wall, 1971

Acrylic, marking ink, and wall-paper on plywood
61.6 x 122.6 cm (24-1/4 x 48-1/4 in.)
EXHIBITION: Toronto, The Isaacs Gallery, 25 January–13 February 1973, (titled *View from Window Above the Double Doors in the West Wall, 1971*).
THE ART BANK, CANADA COUNCIL, OTTAWA, ONTARIO

The text stamped on at the right is by Curnoe, and reads:
"GREY OR GRAY?? ZENITH! A BREEZE HAS COME UP. THE SKY IS OVER-CAST – LIGHT GREY WITH FAINT LINES OF LIGHTER GREY. ITS ABOUT 70 DEGREES OUT. ALL THE LEAVES IN THE TREES ARE MOVING, I CAN HEAR THEM THOUGH THE DOOR UNDER THIS WINDOW IS SHUT. THE WIND IS GETTING STRONGER. THERE IS A HEAVY SENSE OF RELIEF IN THE SKY. THE DARKER GREY CLOUDS ARE MOVING EAST VERY QUICKLY BELOW THE LIGHTER GREY OVERCAST. 5 TO 12 A.M. – SEPTEMBER 15, 1971."
The spelling of the word grey is deliberately English rather than American.

View from the Right Centre Window on the North Wall (August 24, 1971–January 21, 1973)

Oil, marking ink, and wall-paper on plywood, loudspeaker, and magnetic sound tape
182.9 x 122.0 cm (72 x 48 in.); stick with loudspeaker, 48.3 cm (19 in.)
EXHIBITION: Toronto, The Isaacs Gallery, 25 January–13 February 1973, *Greg Curnoe.*
CITY SAVINGS AND TRUST COMPANY, VANCOUVER, BRITISH COLUMBIA

The text stamped on the lower left corner of the window describes the circumstances of the recording of the sound-track:
  "My typewriter is on a table below the window depicted in the painting. On Tuesday, January 16, from 11:30 a.m. to noon and January 18, from 9:30 to 10 a.m. I typed a description of the view out of the window with the tape recorder on and the microphone hung on a nail in the window frame, just above the typewriter."
The profile of the wasp at the top right of the painting, as well as an identical one stamped at the bottom right, were made with a rubber stamp belonging to the artist's older son, Owen. For the other insects, Curnoe used another rubber stamp after a drawing he made especially for the painting.
  The thermometer shown at the left of the window is an advertisement for the Almatex paint company, which produces the bright yellow enamel which Curnoe prefers. It was a gift from his

friends, Don and Bernice Vincent, when he moved to his present studio.

The blue shape appearing at the bottom centre of the painting is a piece of a lamp made of ultramarine blue glass, placed on the window-pane. This piece has the same intense translucent blue as the Bromo bottle shown in the *View of Victoria Hospital, Second Series (February 10, 1969 –March 10, 1971)* in catalogue number 1. This is another colour which Curnoe likes very much.

It is from this window as well that the artist records his journal for the computer.

EXHIBITIONS

(Note: One-man exhibitions by Greg Curnoe and selected group exhibitions are combined; an asterisk indicates a group exhibition.)

*Toronto, The Garrett Gallery, December 1957 (part of a nine-man show).

London, Ontario, Richard E. Crouch Branch Library, 3–30 November 1961. *Exhibition of Things.*

*London, Ontario, Region Gallery, 1962 (?), *Greg Curnoe, Larry Russell.*

*London, Ontario, Region Gallery, March 1963, *Greg Curnoe, Brian Dibb.*

*London, Ontario, The McIntosh Memorial Art Gallery, University of Western Ontario, 26 November–19 December 1962, *Mr. Curnoe and Mrs. Cumming.*

Toronto, Gallery Moos, 12–30 September 1963, *Greg Curnoe.*

Toronto, David Mirvish Gallery, 17 September–6 October 1964, *Greg Curnoe, "STUFF".*

*Regina, Norman Mackenzie Art Gallery, 8–31 October 1964, *John Chambers, Greg Curnoe* (with catalogue).

*London, Ontario, The McIntosh Memorial Art Gallery, University of Western Ontario, 9–27 November 1964, *Imports and Local Art Work Curnoe Urquhart.*

Vancouver, Vancouver Art Gallery, 8–27 February 1966 and Edmonton, Edmonton Art Gallery, 5–31 March 1966, *Paintings by Greg Curnoe* (with catalogues).

Toronto, The Isaacs Gallery, 16 November–5 December 1966, *New Work From Sowesto Greg Curnoe.*

Vancouver, The New Design Gallery, 16 November–5 December 1966, *Recent Collages by Greg Curnoe.*

London, Ontario, 20/20 Gallery, 15 February–5 March 1967, *G. Curnoe's Series.*

Toronto, The Isaacs Gallery, 4–18 April 1967, *G. Curnoe's Time Series.*

*London, Ontario, The McIntosh Memorial Art Gallery, University of Western Ontario, 30 October–11

November 1967, *Chambers and Curnoe Art Exhibit* (with catalogue).

*Regina, Norman Mackenzie Art Gallery, 16 November –17 December 1967, *Statements: 18 Canadian Artists* (with catalogue).

*Paris, Musée national d'art moderne, 12 January – 18 February 1968, *Canada. Art d'aujourd'hui*. The exhibition was shown in Rome, Lausanne, and Brussels (with catalogue).

*Edinburgh, College of Art, Edinburgh International Festival, 18 August–8 September 1968, *Canada 101* (with catalogue).

*Ottawa, The National Gallery of Canada, 1968–1969, *The Heart of London* (a travelling exhibition with catalogue).

Toronto, The Isaacs Gallery, 5–24 February 1969, *Greg Curnoe.*

*London, Ontario, 20/20 Gallery, 22 April–11 May 1969, *The London Survey*. (Group exhibition, including Margo Arris, Don Bellamy, Don Bonham, Jack Chambers, Tom Coulter, Greg Curnoe, Kee Dewdney, Paterson Ewen, Murray Favro, R. Fenwick.)

*Vancouver, Vancouver Art Gallery, 13 January – 8 February 1970, *955,000* (with catalogue).

London, Ontario, The McIntosh Memorial Art Gallery, University of Western Ontario, 2–19 April 1970, *Greg Curnoe Drawings.*

Toronto, The Isaacs Gallery, 29 April–18 May 1970, *Greg Curnoe . . . Collages 1961–70.*

*Montreal, Sir George Williams University and The Saidye Bronfman Centre, 1–17 February 1971, *45° 30′ N–73° 36′ W* (with catalogue).

Toronto, The Isaacs Gallery, 29 April–18 May 1970, *Greg Curnoe Views of Victoria Hospital and Wings over the Atlantic.*

Montreal, Waddington Galleries, 16 November–4 December 1971, *Greg Curnoe.*

London, Ontario, The London House, 1–7 February 1972, *Greg Curnoe – Display of Water Colours Measurements and Clockings.*

Toronto, The Isaacs Gallery, 25 January–13 February 1973, *Greg Curnoe.*

London, Ontario, The Polyglot Gallery, 14 June–5 July 1973, *Greg Curnoe – Watercolours and Drawings.*

Ottawa, The National Gallery of Canada, 1974–1975, *The Great Canadian Sonnet, Drawings by Greg Curnoe* (A travelling exhibition with catalogue).

London, Ontario, The Forest City Art Gallery, 16 November – 4 December 1974, *Greg Curnoe Watercolours.*

Toronto, The Isaacs Gallery, 4–21 February 1975, *Greg Curnoe Recent Watercolours.*

London, Ontario, London Art Gallery, 5–28 September 1975, *Greg Curnoe Some Lettered Works, 1961–1969.*

WRITINGS BY GREG CURNOE
[Arranged in Chronological Order]

[Untitled article dated 15 January 1961], *Region,* no. 1 (1961), n.p.

[Untitled article dated 26 March 1961], *Region,* no. 1 (1961), n.p.

"Statement," *Region,* no. 2 (January 1962), p. 5.

"About Wearing My Dead Grandfather's Glasses," *Region,* no. 3 (1962), n.p.

"Hangover," *Region,* no. 3 (1962), n.p.

"Steering Wheel," *Region,* no. 4 (September 1962), n.p.

"Confessions of an Ex Bicycle Rider," *Region,* no. 5 (February 1963), p. 2.

"Region = Regionalism" [letter to the editor], *The University of Western Ontario Gazette* (15 March 1963), p. 9.

[Untitled], *Region,* no. 6 (1963 ?), n.p.

Walt Redinger: Sculptor, Ed Zelenak: Sculptor, John Boyle: Painter (exhibition catalogue with preface by Greg Curnoe). London, Ontario: The McIntosh Memorial Art Gallery, University of Western Ontario, 1964.

"Selections from 3rd Trip to Montreal," *Region*, no. 7 (June 1964), pp. 32–34.

"Mirrors and Images from the Coke Book," *Alphabet*, no. 9 (November 1964), pp. 43–47.

"Ten artists in search of Canadian art," *Canadian Art*, vol. XXIII, no. 1, issue no. 100 (January 1966), p. 64. See "Greg Curnoe 1936–," by Greg Curnoe.

"Not Leftover Art" [letter to the editor], *The London Free Press* (London, Ontario), 12 July 1966.

[Untitled, editorial], *Region*, no. 8 (summer 1966), n.p.

"Radio Journal" (after March 1970 "Greg Curnoe's Radio Journal"), *20 Cents Magazine*. Regular column by Greg Curnoe, appearing in vol. I: no. 2 (October 1966), n.p.; no. 4 (December 1966), n.p.; no. 5 (January 1967), n.p.; no. 6 (February 1967), n.p.; no. 7 (March 1967), n.p.; no. 8 (April 1967), n.p.; no. 9 (May 1967), n.p.; vol. II: no. 3 (December ? 1967), n.p.; no. 4 (March ? 1968), n.p.; no. 5 (June ? 1968), p. 7; no. 6 (July ? 1968), pp. 33–35; vol. III: nos 3–4 (May 1969), n.p.; no. 10 (December 1969), p. 20 [with title "Radio Journal, Excerpts from Wings Over the Atlantic"]; vol. IV: no. 1 (January 1970), p. 20; no. 3 (March 1970), n.p.; no. 4 (April 1970), n.p.; nos 5–6 (June 1970), n.p.; no. 7 (September 1970), p. 20.

"A Conversation About Mixed Media From New York City as Seen at the University of Western Ontario Nov. 17 and McMaster University, Nov. 12 1966," *20 Cents Magazine*, vol. I, no. 3 (October–November 1966), n.p.

[Untitled, letter to the editor], *20 Cents Magazine*, vol. I, no. 4 (December 1966), n.p.

[Untitled, letter to the editor], *20 Cents Magazine*, vol. I, no. 5 (January 1967), n.p. (Reprint of a letter sent to *The University of Western Ontario Gazette*, 15 March 1963.)

"Boyling Point," *20 Cents Magazine*, vol. I, no. 6 (February 1967), n.p.

"Notes – on the North Wall," *Region*, no. 9 (Spring 1967), n.p.

Statements: 18 Canadian Artists (exhibition catalogue; see texts by Curnoe, pp. 38–42). Regina, Saskatchewan: Norman MacKenzie Art Gallery, 1967.

"N. E. Thing Co. Conference" [article in the column "Radio Journal"], *20 Cents Magazine,* vol. III, nos 5–6 (June 1969), n.p.

"N. E. Thing Co. Conference (Part Two)" [article in the column "Radio Journal"], *20 Cents Magazine,* vol. III, nos 7–8 (October 1969), p. 20.

"Greg Curnoe (from journals written on the C.N.R. on the way to Toronto, 8:55 or so, Wednesday morning, August 13, 1969)," cited on page 25 of an article by Ross Mendes, "The Language of the Eyes Windows and Mirrors," *artscanada,* vol. XXVI, no. 5, issue no. 136/137 (October 1969), pp. 20–25.

"N.E. Thing Co. Conference (Part Three)" [article in the column "Radio Journal"], *20 Cents Magazine,* vol. III, no. 9 (November 1969), p. 20.

"The Coke Book Continued," *Alphabet,* no. 17 (December 1969), pp. 5–9.

Greg Curnoe Canada (exhibition catalogue by Dennis Reid; written for the X Biennial in São Paulo, Brazil, 1969, with texts by Greg Curnoe). Ottawa: The National Gallery of Canada, 1969.

955,000 (exhibition catalogue edited by Lucy Lippard; see texts by Greg Curnoe). Vancouver: Vancouver Art Gallery, 1970.

"The Mothers of Invention – Ron Bowman and Greg Curnoe in Conversation" [article in the column "Radio Journal"], *20 Cents Magazine,* vol. IV, no. 2 (February 1970), n.p.

"Amendments to Continental Refusal/Refus Continental," *20 Cents Magazine,* vol. IV, no. 4 (April 1970), n.p.

Inventions and Perpetual Motion Machines (exhibition catalogue), London, Ontario: 20/20 Gallery, 1970.

"Curnoe on London," *The London Free Press* (London, Ontario), 17 October 1970.

"The most beautiful book in the world," *artscanada,* vol. XXVII, no. 6, issue no. 150/151 (December 1970 – January 1971), pp. 64–65. (A review of the *Economic Atlas of Ontario.* Toronto: 1970.)

[With McFadden, David]. *The Great Canadian Sonnet*. Toronto: Coach House, 1970. Illustrations by Greg Curnoe.

Snore Comix, Bright Things. Toronto: Coach House, 1970. Texts by Greg Curnoe, in collaboration with others.

Nichol, B.P. [ed.]. *The cosmic chef an evening of concrete*. Ottawa: Oberon, 1970. Texts by Greg Curnoe on pp. 7 and 76.

45°30'N – 73°36'W (exhibition catalogue by Gary Coward, Bill Vazan, Arthur Bardo, and Zoe Notkin [ed.]; with texts by Greg Curnoe. Montreal: Sir George Williams University and The Saidye Bronfman Center, 1971.

"Kasabonika – Simmons – Thomas – Curry – Dicy – St. Germain – Patterson – Stansell – Laithwaite etc." (typescript report on popular art for the National Museum of Man, Ottawa, October 1970–March 1971).

"Open Letter to W.O. Twaits, Chairman, Imperial Oil Ltd." (leaflet for a demonstration held in Ottawa, 27 May 1971; co-signed by Greg Curnoe in collaboration with others).

"Notes on Picabia," *artscanada,* vol. XXVIII, no. 4, issue no. 158/159 (August–September 1971), pp. 70, 71.

With Bozak, Bob. "Artists dispute Fanshawe College statement" [letter to the editor], *The London Free Press* (London, Ontario), 2 November 1971.

"Art Purchase" [letter to the editor], *The London Free Press* (London, Ontario), 4 January 1972.

[Review of *The Projector,* by M. Vaughn-James (Toronto: 1971)]; in *The Canadian Forum,* vol. LII, no. 617 (June 1972), pp. 40–41.

[With Théberge, Pierre]. *For Dan Patterson and Arthème St. Germain/Pour Dan Patterson et Arthème St. Germain*. Manifesto of the Association for the Documentation of Neglected Aspects of Culture in Canada, mimeographed sheet, 8 August 1972. Published in *The Review of the Association for the Documentation of Neglected Aspects of Culture in Canada,* vol. I, no. 1. p. 1.

"From the Blue Book/Journals," *Open Letter*, Second
Series, no. 4 (Spring 1973), pp. 94–108.
"Notebook Greg Curnoe," *Proof Only*, vol. i, no. 1
(15 November 1973), pp. 2, 3.
"Canadian Painters" [letter to the editor], *The Globe
and Mail* (Toronto, Ontario), 26 November 1973.
"David McFadden," *The Great Canadian Sonnet
Drawings by Greg Curnoe* (exhibition catalogue).
Ottawa: The National Gallery of Canada, 1974, n.p.
With Bergeron, Léandre. "A Bi-Focus on Barry Lord:
The History of Painting in Canada," *Books in
Canada,* vol. 3, no. 8 (December 1974), pp. 20, 36–38.
"The Dilemma of Provincialism A History of Canadian
Painting," review of Dennis Reid, *A Concise History
of Canadian Painting* (Toronto, 1973) in *The Can-
adian Forum,* vol. 54, no. 648 (February 1975),
pp. 30–32.
"Introduction," *Some Lettered Works by Greg Cur-
noe 1961–1969* (exhibition catalogue), London Art
Gallery, Ontario), 5–28 September 1975.

SELECTED BIBLIOGRAPHY

"An artistic affront to Americans" (editorial), *The
London Free Press* (London, Ontario) 2 April 1968.
p. 6.
Bisset, Bill. *Nobody owns th earth.* Toronto: An-
ansi, 1971.
Bodolai, Joe. "Borderlines in Art and Experience,"
artscanada, vol. xxxi, no. 1, issue no. 188/189
(Spring 1974), pp. 65–81.
Boyle, John B. "Continental Refusal/Refus Conti-
nental." *20 Cents Magazine,* vol. iv, no. 4 (April
1970), n.p.
Chandler, John Noel. "More Words on Curnoe's World-
ly World," *artscanada,* vol. xxvi, no. 2, issue no.
130/131 (April 1969), pp. 3–8.
―――. "Painting 'From Life': Greg Curnoe at the
Isaacs Gallery Ltd," *artscanada,* vol. xxviii, no. 3,

issue no. 156/157 (June–July 1971), p. 75.

———. "Sources are resources: Greg Curnoe's objects, objectives and objections," *artscanada,* vol. xxx, no. 1, issue no. 176/177 (February-March 1973), p. 69.

Cobb, David, "A Man of Involvement," *Toronto Daily Star* (Toronto), 14 September 1963, p. 29.

Coleman, Victor, "Knowing: the surface," *artscanada,* vol. xxix, no. 1, issue no. 164/165 (February–March 1972), pp. 71, 72.

Crawford, Lenore. "Spoofs Reveal Artist, Odd Objects Exhibit Startles Art Lovers," *The London Free Press* (London, Ontario), 4 November 1961.

———."G.Curnoe and K.T.Cumming at the McIntosh Memorial Art Gallery, University of Western Ontario, London," *Canadian Art,* vol. xx, no. 2, issue no. 84 (March–April 1963), pp. 86, 87.

———. "Londoners step up invasion of Montreal Art Galleries," *The London Free Press* (London, Ontario), 4 April 1964.

———. "Galleries Like Works of Londoner," *The London Free Press* (London, Ontario), 30 September 1964.

———. "Urquhart, Curnoe exhibit a mixture of color, vitality, humor," *The London Free Press* (London, Ontario), 14 November 1964.

———. "Artist Curnoe more 'Involved' than ever," *The London Free Press* (London, Ontario), 3 December 1966.

———. "The Spasms," *The London Free Press* (London, Ontario), 3 February 1968, p. 35.

———. "Before storm," *The London Free Press* (London, Ontario), 30 March 1968.

———. "Curnoe art dominates new show," *The London Free Press* (London, Ontario), 21 July 1970.

———. "Curnoe displays art in Toronto," *The London Free Press* (London, Ontario), 20 March 1971.

———. "Canada buys Curnoe work," *The London Free Press* (London, Ontario), 14 August 1971.

———. "Curnoe 'on the spot' water-colors show 'first' for old hotel," *The London Free Press* (London, Ontario), 2 February 1972.

————. "Curnoe reveals superb new talent," *The London Free Press* (London, Ontario), 25 June 1973.

"Curnoe – A File Interview," *File,* vol. II, nos 1–2 (April–May 1973), pp. 46, 47, 61.

"Curnoe at the Front," *Georgia Straight* (Vancouver), 6–13 June 1974.

Dault, Gary Michael. "Heart of London," *artscanada,* vol. XXV, no. 4, issue no. 122/123 (October–November 1968), p. 43.

————. "Greg Curnoe's love of bicycles expressed in beautiful paintings" (*Toronto Star*), 7 February 1975.

Davis, Rae. "The Life of death in London," *Canadian Art,* vol. XXIII, no. 3, issue no. 102 (July 1966), pp. 20–25, 50–51.

Hale, Barry. "Stick around and work with what's around you," *Saturday Night,* vol. LXXXV, no. 1, issue no. 3499 (January 1970), pp. 25–29.

Harris, Marjorie. "Nihilist Spasm Band," *artscanada,* vol. XXV, no. 2, issue no. 118/119 (June 1968), pp. 6, 7.

Kidd, Bruce. "Bruce Kidd interviews Greg Curnoe," *The Canadian Forum,* vol. LIII, no. 631 (August 1973), pp. 22–30.

Lord, Barry. "Painters Became Politically Aware in '68," *Kitchener-Waterloo Record* (Kitchener-Waterloo, Ontario), 28 December 1968.

————. "What London, Ontario has that everywhere else needs," *Art in America,* vol. LVII, no. 5 (September–October 1969), pp. 103–105.

————. *The History of Painting in Canada: Toward a People's Art.* Toronto: N.C. Press, 1974.

McFadden, David. *The Great Canadian Sonnet.* Toronto: Coach House, 1970. Illustrated by Greg Curnoe.

————. "Concerning Greg Curnoe, Artist," *The Great Canadian Sonnet Drawings by Greg Curnoe* (exhibition catalogue). Ottawa: The National Gallery of Canada, 1974.

McKenzie, Robert C. "Beaver kosmos: A Narrowminded

Review," *20 Cents Magazine,* vol. I, no. 8 (April 1967), n.p.

———. "Greg Curnoe's Connexions," *20 Cents Magazine,* vol. IV, no. 3 (March 1970), n.p.

McPherson, Hugo. "Greg Curnoe's Shorthand," *20 Cents Magazine,* vol. I, no. 6 (February 1967), n.p.

Mendes, Ross. "The language of the eyes – Windows and Mirrors," *artscanada,* vol. XXVI, no. 5, issue no. 136/137 (October 1969), pp. 20–25.

Oille, Jennifer. "Greg Curnoe at the Isaacs Gallery," *Only Paper Today,* vol. II, no. 6 (March 1975), p. 2.

Parker, Harley. "Greg Curnoe's paintings: Moos Gallery,Toronto (September 12–October 2),"*Alphabet,* no. 7 (December 1963), pp. 87–89.

Pratten, Art. "Note from the 'Art Editor'," *20 Cents Magazine,* vol. I, no. 8 (April 1967), n.p.

Pringle, Douglas. "The Great Canadian Sonnet," *artscanada,* vol. XXVII, no. 4, issue no. 146/147 (August 1970), pp. 71, 72.

Rabinowitch, Royden. "Nihilists Co-operate," *20 Cents Magazine,* vol. I, no. 4 (December 1966), n.p.

Rans, Geoffrey. "A Word (Sotto Voce) About the Region: inside my picket fence in London, Ontario," *20 Cents Magazine,* vol. II, no. 1 (January 1967), n.p.

———. "20/20 Gallery: A Report and a Prediction," *20 Cents Magazine,* vol. I, no. 8 (April 1967), n.p.

Reaney, James. *John Chambers, Greg Curnoe* (introduction to exhibition catalogue, Regina, Norman Mackenzie Art Gallery, 1964).

———."Role of the inscription in painting," *Canadian Art,* vol. XXIII, no. 4, issue no. 103 (October 1966), pp. 41–45.

Reid, Dennis. *Greg Curnoe Canada* (exhibition catalogue for the X Biennial in São Paulo, Brazil. Ottawa: The National Gallery of Canada, 1969).

———. *A Concise History of Canadian Painting.* Toronto: Oxford University Press, 1973.

Robillard, Yves. "L'affaire de la murale de l'aéroport de Dorval," *La Presse* (Montreal), 6 April 1968.

Rockman, Arnold. "Greg Curnoe at the Gallery Moos, Toronto," *Canadian Art,* vol. XXI, no. 1, issue no.

89 (January–February 1964), p. 10.

"69". "The object Was to Paint (Print?) 24 Panels, One An Hour For 24 Hours, From 12:00 a.m. Wednesday, December 14th, to 12:00 a.m. Thursday, December 15th. The Panels Were 10 by 10 Sheets of Tin Plate With Lapped Edges," *20 Cents Magazine,* vol. I, no. 4 (December 1966), n.p.

Théberge, Pierre. "Confessions of a Nihilist Spasm Band Addict," *artscanada,* vol. XXVI, no. 6, issue no. 138/139 (December 1969), pp. 67, 68.

––––. "Sixty drawings by Greg Curnoe for *The Great Canadian Sonnet* by David McFadden '. . .beautiful . . . like the chance encounter of a sewing machine and an umbrella on a dissecting table' (Lautréamont)," *The Great Canadian Sonnet Drawings by Greg Curnoe* (exhibition catalogue), Ottawa: The National Gallery of Canada, 1974.

Thompson, David. "A Canadian Scene: 3," *Studio International,* vol. CLXXVI, no. 906 (December 1968), pp. 241–245.

Wallace, Helen. "Remove objectionable Curnoe airport art," *The London Free Press* (London, Ontario), 28 March 1968, p. 31.

––––. "Anti-American work by Curnoe removed from Dorval Airport mural," *The London Free Press* (London, Ontario), 29 March 1968, pp. 1, 10

––––. "While controversy rages," *The London Free Press* (London, Ontario), 30 March 1968.

"The Weekly Interview, Greg Curnoe (Part I)," *The London Weekly* (London, Ontario), 16 July 1968.

"The Weekly Interview, Greg Curnoe (Part II)," *The London Weekly* (London, Ontario), 23 July 1968.

Woodman, Ross. "Greg Curnoe" [mimeographed introduction for the exhibition *Greg Curnoe Series,* London, Ontario, 20/20 Gallery, 15 February – 5 March 1967].

––––. "London (Ont.): a new regionalism," *arts canada,* vol. XXIV, no. 8–9,issue no. 111/112 (August September 1967), insert, n.p.

––––."London: regional liberation front," *The Globe and Mail* (Toronto), 13 December 1969.

FOTOGRAFIE
PHOTOGRAPHIES
PHOTOGRAPHS

Galleria Nazionale del Canada/Galerie nationale du Canada/The National Gallery of Canada, Ottawa: Fotografie del testo del cat. no. 1, figura III; photographies du texte du cat. n° 1, fig. III; photographs of text of cat. no. 1, fig. III.

Ayriss, Toronto: no. 2, 3, 4, 5, 6.

John Evans, Ottawa: no. 1.

André Nufer, Design Associates, London. Ontario: copertina/couverture/cover.

Don Vincent, London, Ontario: fig. I.

Lyle Wachovsky, Toronto: fig. II, no. 7, 8.

HANNO COLLABORATO
COLLABORATEURS
CREDITS

Disegno/présentation/design: Eiko Emori
Copertina/couverture/cover: Greg Curnoe
Stampa/impression/printing: Dollco Printing

Copertina: Lo studio di Greg Curnoe, febbraio 1974.
Couverture: L'atelier de Greg Curnoe, février 1974.
Cover: Greg Curnoe's studio, February 1974.